Are the Rich Necessary?

Are the Rich Necessary?

*Great Economic Arguments
and How They Reflect Our
Personal Values*

Hunter Lewis

Axios Press
P.O. Box 118
Mount Jackson, VA 22842
888.542.9467   info@axiospress.com

Distributed by NATIONAL BOOK NETWORK.

ISBN: 978-0-9753662-0-2
Library of Congress Control Number: 2007923586

Publisher's Cataloging-in-Publication Data

Lewis, Hunter.
    Are the rich necessary? : great economic arguments and how they reflect our personal values / Hunter Lewis.
        p.   cm.
    Includes bibliographical references and index.
    LCCN 2007923586
    ISBN-13: 978-0-9753662-0-2
    ISBN-10: 0-9753662-0-3

    1. Economics. 2. Social values.   I. Title.

HB71.L49 2007   330
                                QBI07-600117

Contents

Part One

The Central
Economic Problem

1

Why Are We Still
So Poor?

IF YOU PUT $10 IN A BANK ACCOUNT and earn 3%
interest, the money will double every twenty-five
years. Even after a long lifetime, you might have
only $30 or $40 dollars. "No way to get rich," you are
thinking.

But humanity goes on. Imagine that the bank account
kept on doubling every quarter century for 1,000 years.
The original $10 would then have grown to a sum worth
over two times the world's total wealth today.

Compounding money over long periods of time
produces fantastic results. So why has humanity not
done better? The reason is simple. Throughout human
history, capital has been created, capital has been

destroyed, over and over. Compounding has hardly had a chance to start, much less reach the magic of multiplying large numbers.

There are a variety of reasons for this: natural disasters such as disease and weather-related famine, war, and other human follies. But there has also been almost complete intellectual confusion about how to organize ourselves to end poverty and deprivation.

We also know, through simple intuition, that it is not enough to find the right answer. We must agree on the answer. Societies do not become rich simply by preserving and growing their capital. They become rich by cooperating. The more cooperation, the more potential to preserve, invest, and grow capital. There is an irony in this. We need to cooperate. But, almost at once, we start to argue about how we might best go about cooperating.

2

The Appeal of Science

ONE WAY TO try to overcome this initial obstacle, the difficulty in deciding how best to go about cooperating, is to see if we can develop economics into a science. A scientific approach would separate truth from error and help us reach agreement.

But can economics be a science? Is wealth creation like building an engine or a bridge, something that will follow formal rules, as soon as we discover the rules? Or is wealth creation more like raising children, a task for which there are no formal rules, at least no rules that fit every occasion and every child?

If the economic problem is a scientific one, it can be solved. If a non-scientific one, it can only be managed, not solved. In the latter case, we will have to rely on our judgment, in particular we will have to rely on value judgments.

Economist Milton Friedman thought that economics could be a science. He spoke for many of his colleagues in the 1950s when he wrote that "Economics is, or can be, an 'objective' science, in precisely the same sense as any of the physical sciences."[1]

Unfortunately, there are important reasons why a scientific approach to economics may not work. To begin with, the ultimate subject matter in economics is human behavior, and human beings are notoriously unpredictable. Today we want this, tomorrow we want the opposite, and there may not be much "rhyme or reason" about it.

Our unpredictability is only one problem. There is another major one. If we watch an apple fall from a tree, our watching has no effect on the apple. But if we watch people, the lessons we learn may change our behavior or even the behavior of the people we are watching.

Here's an example. Assume that people study stock market history and decide that stocks are the best and the safest place to put their money. What will they do then?

Naturally they will buy more and more stocks. But, by doing so together, they will raise prices dramatically, and this will make the stocks more and more risky. Eventually, almost all the potential buyers will already have bought, so that people who must sell (such as retirees) will have no one left to whom to sell. At that point, prices will collapse, leaving millions of investors poor and bewildered.

This is not a hypothetical example. Something similar happened in the great American stock market crashes of 1929, 1973, and 2000. The lesson here is clear: just when we all decide that something in economics is "true," it may cease to be true.

3

Economic Arguments

WHETHER WE LIKE it or not, economics is unlikely to become a science, in the same sense that physics or chemistry are sciences. But that does not mean that there are no economic answers. We must find them and we do.

In the first place, we develop guiderules based on our life experiences. Sometimes these guiderules are highly contextual, even paradoxical, as in the motto, "Moderation in all things, even in moderation."

We also form ideals, and try to temper those ideals with common sense. We change our stance as the times change. Above all, we argue.

Many economics textbooks downplay arguments. They do not want to leave an impression that nothing is settled, that the entire field is in a state of chaos. This is understandable. As noted earlier, we cannot create wealth without cooperating. And we cannot cooperate if we are always fighting over who is right.

Nevertheless, it may be better to acknowledge forthrightly that economics is, now and always, an intellectual, moral, and material battlefield. On the positive side, this means that economics, properly presented, is rarely dull, because there is nothing more exciting than entering a battlefield.

In any case, the remainder of this book will present a series of fundamental economic arguments. These arguments are fundamental in the sense that they underlie many other, perhaps most other economic quarrels. For example, the question "Are the rich necessary?" underlies many of the most contentious issues about how the government should intervene (or not intervene) in the economy.

In presenting these fundamental economic arguments, the author of this book has tried to avoid taking sides. Only the reader can judge the success of this effort to stand back from the economic battlefield, and the verdict is not likely to be kind. But, in every case, both sides of the argument are covered, first one side, then the other. To borrow super-lawyer Robert Strauss's quip, the object has been to "teach it flat and teach it round" and then let the reader choose.

As the book progresses through the arguments, some of the debating points may appeal to our emotions, some to logic, some to "common sense," which usually reflects our practical experience. Some may be simple, others complex. If a point of view is complex, it may get more space.

Unequal space for contesting points of view may strike some readers as a betrayal of the author's intention to try to avoid taking sides. Should not the "equal time" doctrine applied to commercial broadcasts of political debates in the U.S. also apply here? But, in this case, we are not dealing with candidate A versus candidate B. We are dealing with ideas, some simple, some complex. A rigid, Procrustean, one-size-fits-all approach will not help us to understand them. In any case, simple (and brief) ideas are often more persuasive than complex (and wordy) ones.

It goes without saying that the author of this book does have his own ideas like anyone else. Some of these ideas are laid out in the last chapter. In particular, I would like to expand the part of the economy that is neither "private" (owned by individuals) nor "public" (owned or controlled by government). That is, I would like to expand the charitable or non-profit sector, something that could easily be accomplished by changes in the tax code. My hope is that this approach would help reduce the bitter quarrels that continually rage over the degree of government control of the economy.

But, as stated above, the principal purpose of this book is not to propagate a particular set of ideas. It is instead to present a variety of conflicting economic ideals, ideas, and arguments, so that the reader can better understand the issues, and then decide for himself or herself.

So many of the choices that voters in a democracy face require at least some knowledge of economics, yet it is not easy to get the issues in clear focus. I hope that this book helps at least some voters to clarify their own thinking. Voters should also understand that the way the government, representing us, responds to these issues will directly affect their jobs, raises, promotions, and, in general, all their economic opportunities.

One final point should be made before embarking on the arguments. People tend to be very passionate, if not about economics, then about some of the issues surrounding economics, issues such as whether the rich should pay more in taxes. It is easy, in the midst of all the passion, to conclude that one's opponents are selfish, evil, or perhaps just "dumb."

I have found many an economic idea to be, if not "dumb," then at least illogical or impractical. But, even so, more often than not I have found myself sympathizing with the ideals that underlie it. Indeed, I believe that if we take the trouble to look beneath the surface of clashing economic ideas, we will generally find some ideals on all sides that are inspiring, and others that are at least worthy of respect.

Part Two

The Rich

4

Are the Rich Necessary?—No

O

N ONE LEVEL, this might seem to be a foolish question. Large-scale human societies have never been run on a truly share-and-share-alike basis. Even the Russian Communists, who espoused such principles, completely failed to live up to them. If the rich have always been with us, they probably always will be with us, so why concern ourselves further?

In fact, however, the role of the rich is and should be hotly debated. People referred to as "egalitarians" or "equalitarians" (we shall use the latter term) want to get rid of them, or at least reduce the extremes of wealth and poverty. If we cannot eliminate the rich entirely, they say, can we not at least tax the rich to help the poor?

The equalitarian case against the rich may be summarized as a series of arguments:

Argument 1: The rich are essentially parasites.

A student working as a summer farmhand explains:

> I had been on the baler all day, the usual ten hours. . . . The Nevada sun was hot, and the work was dusty. As usual, Mr. Phelps [the farm owner] had been cruising around, checking on us from his air-conditioned, white Lincoln Continental. We were sweating for just over minimum wage. He wasn't working, but he was making the profits. It . . . didn't . . . look fair . . . to me.[2]

Argument 2: Wealth causes poverty; without rich people there would be no poor people.

Political commentator George Will thinks this argument absurd: "People are not hungry in Bombay [now Mumbai] because people are well-fed in Boston."[3]

But Argument 2 cannot be dismissed so readily. The fact remains that if the top one percent of American earners gave away half their net income after tax to charity, and those funds went directly to the American poor, poverty as defined by the government would be eliminated. It is true that these same funds spread globally would barely dent the problem. There is an especially acute moral dilemma sorting out national versus international claims, since the global poor have so much less than the American poor. But the observation that desperately poor people need more money, and that others are awash in money, is indisputable.

Argument 3: The problem is not simply that very rich people do not share adequately with the poor.

The larger problem is that the rich steal from or exploit the poor, that, as Proudhon said, "property is theft."[4]

The Book of Isaiah in the Bible tells us that "The spoil of the poor is in your houses; what mean ye that ye crush my people, And grind the face of the poor? Saith the LORD, God of hosts."[5]

Each generation rediscovers this idea anew. As heiress Abby Rockefeller, a great-grandchild of John D. Rockefeller, Sr., has written:

> That riches and poverty were interwoven,
> that one fed on the other, that the many suf-
> fered because of the few; that good and bad
> fortune were inextricably linked—this was
> new for me. It was compelling.[6]

The notion that rich people and their corporate agents grind poor people into the ground, exploit them, steal from them, deny them decent living standards or healthcare, or otherwise abuse them, may be articulated at the national as well as the personal level. Monsignor Alfonso Lopez Trujillo, Secretary General of the Latin American Bishops' Conference, has written that "the United States and Canada are rich because the peoples of Latin America are poor. They have built their wealth on top of us."[7]

Julius Nyerere, long-time president of Tanzania and respected leader of the "Third World" during the U.S.–Soviet Cold War, suggested that the economically advanced "First World" faced a choice between reparations and revolution:

> In one world, as in one state, when I am rich because you are poor, . . . the transfer of wealth from the rich to the poor is a matter of right. It is not an appropriate matter of charity.[8]

Ronald J. Sider, equalitarian author of *Rich Christians in an Age of Hunger*, agrees with Nyerere's diagnosis but not his prescription of rich countries giving away far more money. Sider thinks that it would be better for the West to acknowledge that its wealth has been taken from others, then reduce its need for wealth by leading a simpler, less extravagant lifestyle.[9]

5

Are the Rich Necessary?—Yes

THE EQUALITARIAN CASE against rich people is compelling. Questions of exploitation aside, why shouldn't the rich share what they have with the poor? But it is time to turn to other voices and listen to what they have to say:

Argument 4: Our economy needs rich people precisely because they are rich.

The basic idea is as follows. Everyone—rich, middle class, or poor—benefits from an expanding economy. An economy expands by becoming more productive. We become more productive by learning how to produce more and more, better and better, with the same number of workers. Productivity increases as we give workers better tools. In order to afford these tools, we need to put away some of what we make each year. That is, we need to save, so that we can invest the savings in the tools we need.

The problem then arises: how to induce people to save? The poor cannot be expected to save, because they need every dollar for basic needs such as food and shelter. Middle class people will save something for emergencies, children's education, or old age. But they have many immediate needs and desires, and in any case their savings will eventually be consumed, especially after retirement. The rich, however, are different. They have so much money that, in aggregate, they simply cannot spend it all. They are, in effect, forced to save.

As economist Wilhelm Ropke has explained:

> The notion of the rich gluttonously stuffing themselves is inexact, the stomach capacity of most individuals being approximately the same. Of course, the larger ... a [person's] income, the greater will be [the] consumption of luxury goods. . . . But even such luxury wants [cannot] absorb the whole of a very large income. The result is that the unspent portion of the very large income is saved.[10]

Historian Paul Johnson comments further:

> As people who acquire riches quickly discover, once you are well-fed, clothed and

> housed, you have to spend your money on
> competitive ostentation—or save it. Either
> choice brings problems and worries. . . . [In
> any case,] amassing wealth has nothing to do
> with happiness.[11]

Of course, one can decide that the state will take over the saving and investment function by taxing away the rich person's wealth. But the problem quickly arises that the state, unlike rich people, never runs out of things to spend money on. Moreover, public officials are like other people: they prefer to spend rather than save, and there is no way to compel governments to become savers, since governments by definition control the social instruments of compulsion. In the case of the Soviet Union, the government chose to spend larger and larger sums on weapons, and that money could not simultaneously be used for productive investment.

Just how important is savings and investment? In the first place, it is precisely the failure to save and invest, and to protect savings, that has kept humanity so poor. In the second place, it may be argued that our very lives depend on the steady increase in our capital. As economic writer Henry Hazlitt has pointed out:

> Aside from the notorious fact that the con-
> dition of the masses is enormously better
> than it was . . . before the Industrial Revo-
> lution . . . , there is the still more notorious

fact that the population of the world since then has increased [many-fold]. It was capital accumulation that made this possible. This means that ... [many] of us owe our very existence to the savings and investments of our forebears.[12]

Argument 5: There cannot be too much saving if it is invested properly.

Some economists have responded that the rich save too much and spend too little, that jobs would be more plentiful and everyone would be better off if money came out from under mattresses and circulated more freely. This would be true if the rich really kept their money hidden in mattresses. But the lure of earning interest or capital gains usually ensures that money circulates whether it is spent or saved. If a rich person buys a yacht, this creates jobs for yacht-makers. But if, instead, the rich person buys some shares of stock from a company, and the company then uses the money to build a plant, there will also be more jobs for plant construction workers.

In terms of immediate new jobs created, spending and investment are equivalent. But there the similarity stops because investment spurs productivity, which leads to economic growth, which creates new jobs for the future.

Henry Hazlitt again:

Contrary to age-old prejudices, the wealth of the rich is not the cause of the poverty of the poor, but helps to alleviate that poverty. No matter whether it is their intention or not, almost anything that the rich can legally do tends to help the poor. The spending of the rich gives employment to the poor. But the saving of the rich, and their investment of these savings in the means of production, gives just as much employment, and in addition makes that employment constantly more productive and more highly paid, while it also constantly increases and cheapens the production of necessities and amenities for the masses.[13]

The rich should of course be directly charitable in the conventional sense to people who because of illness, disability or other misfortune cannot take employment or earn enough. Conventional forms of private charity should constantly be extended. But . . . those who truly want to help the poor will not spend their days in organizing protest marches.[14]

The most effective charity on the part of the rich is to live simply, to avoid extravagance and ostentatious display, to save and invest so as to provide more people with increasingly productive jobs, and to provide the masses with an ever-greater abundance of the necessities and amenities of life.[15]

Argument 6: The rich have vital work to do too, and if they shirk it or do it badly, they will lose their money.

A superficial reading of Hazlitt might suggest that the rich are rather like the modern, constitutional monarchs of Britain. Their job is simply to be there, they can be as passive as they wish, although they can be more virtuous by living simply and restraining a taste for luxury, avoiding useless status displays, and especially refraining from destroying wealth wantonly or burying it in graves, as has been commonly done throughout human history. But this would be a misreading.

Hazlitt expects more of the rich. He expects them to work, preferably to work intelligently and hard, but at least intelligently, and to earn their keep, not only by saving and investing, but by investing wisely. This can sometimes be accomplished by hiring others to make decisions, in which case the rich are investing in other people rather than directly in businesses. But however the rich do their investing, it is the results that count. If the present guardians of social savings invest well, as measured by business profits and economic growth, they deserve to stay rich or become even richer. If they invest poorly, the system will quickly take their savings away, as it should.

The problem of quality, as opposed to quantity, of investment lies at the heart of economics. But it has received surprisingly little attention from modern economists. Only a rare text focuses on the importance of making sound investments, even though quality arguably matters much more than quantity of investment in producing economic growth.

Economics textbooks generally do recognize the importance of innovation and risk-taking in the economy, which is another important facet of rich people's investment job. Governments can also, of course, supply risk capital, but rich people arguably do it better because their investment decisions are less politicized, their cash is less bureaucratized, and their sheer numbers increase the odds that a long-shot, but ultimately good, idea will get funded.

Finally, rich people are supposed to provide general management for businesses, including cost and quality controls, again either directly as owners and executives, or, indirectly, by choosing and supervising managers. It is a major error that so many societies have tried to develop themselves while warring against their own most experienced and motivated developers, the rich.

Argument 7: The charge that the rich can only make others richer through a "trickle-down" process is false.

Equalitarians often mock their opponents for espousing a "trickle-down" theory of economics, one that wants to make the rich richer as the first step in making others richer. Mary Landrieu, Democratic senator from Louisiana, thinks that "This whole [idea that wealth will] 'trickle down' is hogwash."[16]

The first question to be asked here is whether this is what opponents of equalitarianism are really saying, that the rich must benefit first in order for others to follow. Thinker and commentator Irving Kristol describes "trickle down" as a "nasty phrase" for what is really a socially desirable process, but agrees that "the businessman ... is very likely to reap visible 'disproportionate' rewards, while the benefits of his activity gradually and indirectly 'trickle down' to the rest of us."[17]

Economist Thomas Sowell sharply disagrees and regards the very concept of "trickle down" as erroneous. As he says:

> It is nonsense to [describe economic growth as] "trickling down" [from the rich] . . . . The [rich person's] investment has to happen first, and workers have to be hired and paid first, before the investor has any hope of reaping any gains. Since capital gains come last, not first, they do not "trickle down."[18]

Argument 8: What would actually happen if the government decided to seize rich people's assets entirely in order to give them to the poor?

The rich hold most of their wealth in the form of bonds, stocks, or real estate, all of which rise and fall in price depending on market demand for them. If word spread that wealth would be redistributed, buyers of these assets would disappear and prices plummet. Later, after assets were seized, they would have to be sold in order to provide cash to distribute. But these sales, with few offsetting buyers, would quickly prove impossible. Meanwhile, companies, unsure of the future flow of savings, would stop investing, with the result that many people would lose their jobs. In effect, then, the great risk of all redistribution schemes, however well intentioned, is that savings and investment, that is, the capital underlying the economy, are simply destroyed. Even if the rich voluntarily decided to sell their assets in order to distribute cash to the poor, the same sequence of events would unfold.

Argument 9: Response

Even *if* the rich do currently play an indispensable role, surely no one with ordinary human sympathies can feel completely comfortable about the huge disparities in wealth that exist in every society. If the government has not shown itself to be a reliable or competent saver and investor, and therefore a suitable substitute for the rich, might there be some other alternative? This question will be addressed later in the book. For now, we will look at the problem of the rich from a somewhat different angle and ask whether rich people are compatible with democracy.

Part Three

The Rich in a Democracy

6

Are the Rich Compatible with Democracy?—No

Argument 1: The rich stand in the way of democracy and often intentionally thwart it.

GREAT WEALTH AND DEMOCRACY are incompatible for many reasons. To begin with, the rich use their money to buy political influence and thereby subvert the democratic process. As democracy weakens, the rule of law is increasingly flouted, and the income gap between rich and poor widens further. George Garret, writer, official poet laureate of the state of Virginia, and University of Virginia professor, has described the process:

> White collar and corporate crime . . . and the
> gap between rich and poor . . . [are] seriously
> compromising the plausibility of a demo-
> cratic government. Our votes do not count
> very much, yours and mine.[19]

Argument 2: We need complete democracy.

The problem in a nutshell is that one cannot have political democracy without economic democracy. The two go hand in hand, together represent complete democracy, and complete democracy is exactly what we need. As economist Paul McCulley has said, "Democracy starts with the socialist notion of one person, one vote. Yes, socialist notion!"[20]

Yet capitalism proceeds on the contrary notion of one dollar (or euro or yen), one vote, which means that rich people have a vastly disproportionate say. One person, one vote and one dollar, one vote are obviously incompatible notions. Incompatibility breeds tension, and the tension can only be relieved by abandoning democracy or by making wealth more equal, so that people have a more equivalent number of dollars.

7

Are the Rich Compatible with Democracy?—Yes

Argument 3: On close inspection, free-market arrangements are more democratic than they at first appear.

OR EXAMPLE, TAKE the assertion that the one dollar, one vote free-market system gives the rich a disproportionate voice as consumers. Is this actually true? In the first place, when the rich save and invest, they are not consuming, so they bring fewer dollars into the consumer market than might be supposed. In the second place, the non-rich vastly outnumber the rich. Consequently, the dollars of non-rich consumers outnumber the dollars of rich consumers. Under these circumstances, it is the non-rich "voters" who actually control the direction of production.

Once we understand that non-rich, average consumers actually control the direction of production, we will then have to reconsider the respective roles of employers and employees. If employees, acting as consumers, are in fact the real bosses, then employers must be the real employees.

This idea, that workers in a fully competitive market economy are really working for themselves, is not a new one. British economist Edwin Cannan observed in 1928 that "[Some] try to convince the wage-earners that they are working not for the public and not for the consumers of the things or services which they produce, but for the capitalist employer, [but this is just] ... sour propaganda."[21]

Cannan's thesis may be disputed at a number of levels. It certainly looks as if the producer is the boss—after all, whose signature is on the paycheck? Beatrice Potter, who along with her husband Sidney Webb led early-twentieth-century British socialism, wrote in her memoirs that "In the business of my father everybody had to obey the orders issued by my father, the boss. He alone had to give orders, but to him nobody gave any orders."[22]

In response, economist Ludwig von Mises pointed out that "This is a very short-sighted view. Orders were given to her father by the consumers, by the buyers. Unfortunately [Potter] could not see these orders. ..."[23]

Von Mises continues:

> Descriptive terms which people use are often
> quite misleading. In talking about modern cap-
> tains of industry and leaders of big business, for
> instance, they call a man a "chocolate king" or
> a "cotton king" or an "automobile king." Their
> use of such terminology implies that they see
> practically no difference between the modern
> heads of industry and those feudal kings, dukes
> or lords of earlier days. But the difference is in
> fact very great, for a chocolate king does not
> rule at all, he serves. This "king" must stay in
> the good graces of his subjects, the consumers;
> he loses his "kingdom" as soon as he is no lon-
> ger in a position to give his customers better
> service and provide it at lower cost than others
> with whom he must compete.[24]

The notion of consumer sovereignty has been disputed on other grounds. One point of view holds that
most consumers are too ignorant, even about their
own needs, too easily led and manipulated by propaganda and advertising, to be described as bosses. Is it
not an outright deception to refer to consumers as
bosses when they are being dragged onto a treadmill
of relentless work and endless debts to satisfy appe-
tites that are often unhealthy and have been viciously
inflamed to fatten the coffers of the rich? Ludwig von
Mises again offers a rejoinder:

> The moralists' and sermonizers' critique . . . misses the point. It is not the fault of the entrepreneurs that the consumers—the people . . . —prefer liquor to Bibles and detective stories to serious books. . . . The entrepreneur does not make greater profits in selling "bad" things than in selling "good" things. His profits are the greater the better he . . . provid[es] the consumers with those things they ask for most intensely.[25]

Argument 4: Rich people should not be described as "bosses," but rather as "trustees."

If we accept the argument that average consumers direct the economy, that they are the ultimate bosses, we are then left with the question of how best to define the role of the nominal bosses, the rich business owners and company chief executives. Von Mises has admonished us that we should not call them kings, barons, titans, and such like, but then what should we call them? Surely they cannot really be described as employees. Economist Abba Lerner suggests the term "social agents":

> People who earn millions of dollars . . . are, in fact, acting as agents for society. It is as if the wealth belonged to society at large, and they were merely looking after it on behalf of the rest of us.[26]

Wilhelm Ropke offers the terms "public servant" and "trustee":

> [Business owners] really fulfill the function of social officials, who are selected on the strict principle of performance, who are responsible for the good management of the means of production and for this get paid a sum that, all in all, is probably less than the pay of officials in a socialist state in relation to their performance. . . .[27] Looked at in this light, people like Henry Ford are really public servants who administer our productive resources after the manner of trustees and who, if their trusteeship is bad, undergo the immediate and heavy punishment of financial loss.[28]

Terms such as social agent, public servant, and trustee may seem fanciful when applied to the rich. The rich themselves would surely be puzzled by such claims. Yet von Mises argues strongly that Lerner and Ropke are right: "In the market society the proprietors of capital and land . . . must serve the consumers in order to have any advantage from what is their own."[29]

Argument 5: As Ropke, von Mises, and Hazlitt have emphasized, the acid test for the idea of the business leader as servant is that there must be downward as well as upward mobility for the

rich, that the consumer must be able to give, but also to take away.

If this condition does not exist, then rich people hold their wealth illegitimately, and do not deserve the support of democrats.

The evidence of downward mobility for companies clearly exists, but what about for rich people? Here we have at least the following:

- ■■ The U.S. Internal Revenue Service reports that over a nine-year-period since it began compiling statistics on the 400 highest-paying taxpayers, only 1% of the names have been on the list every year;[30]

- ■■ *Forbes* Magazine reports that over a twenty-two-year period since it began compiling a list of the 400 richest Americans (assets, not income), only 50 individuals or 13% have managed to stay on the list for the full period;[31]

- ■■ Glenn Hubbard, a Treasury Department official and later chairman of the President's Council of Economic Advisors, looked at the top 1% of U.S. taxpayers at the start and end of a ten-year period, and found that over a third fell out of the top group and that the initial top group's average income fell by 11%.[32]

Argument 6: As we have seen, a free-market economy is democratic because it is run by average consumers who can hire and fire the rich at will. But this is not the end of the story.

The free-market democratic system of one dollar, one vote is actually superior to the political democratic system of one person, one vote. Indeed, it is, in the final analysis, more democratic.

This argument runs as follows. In a consumer democracy, if I vote for product X, I get product X. If you vote for product Y, you get product Y. This is in sharp contrast to a political democracy, where only one candidate can win, and no one vote counts for much in the final result.

There is even a question whether political elections actually reflect the will of the people. Let us assume a hypothetical election in which 60% of the eligible voters vote, eligible voters represent half the population of the country, state, or city, and the successful candidate carries 60% of the vote. In that case, only 18% of the people have chosen the successful candidate (even fewer presumably agree with all the candidates positions), yet this decision must be accepted by all under force of law. By contrast, a free-market economic democracy counts votes proportionally, not winner-take-all. We get exactly as much of candidate (product) A as the voters want, exactly as much of candidate (product) B as the voters want, and so forth, with both majority and minority will fully expressed, and no one overruled.

Argument 7: Response.

This idea of the rich as "social agents" and "trustees" is just delusional fantasy. Rich people amass wealth for selfish, not altruistic reasons. It is perverse to call an economic system "democratic" when poor people have so few votes, while a single rich person may have billions of them.

Part Four

Profit-making

8

Are Private Profits Necessary?—No

PRIVATE BUSINESS PROFITS are the wellsprings of private wealth. Equalitarians therefore take a dim view of private profit-making, and offer the following arguments:

Argument 1: Private enterprise pits owners and workers against each other in a ceaseless struggle, a struggle that is ultimately self-defeating for everyone.

Businesses may create profits by overcharging consumers. A more common tactic is to underpay employees. The truth is that owners and their profits can only thrive at workers' expense and vice versa. In this conflict, owners have the whip hand because workers cannot afford to lose their jobs, although labor unions have helped level the playing field.

In the end, however, everyone loses, because the system suffers from a fatal defect. The profit system, insofar as it limits workers' incomes, also limits workers' ability to buy consumer goods. If a more just distribution between owners and workers could be achieved, the economy would boom as workers spent their new income.

In the short run, the best way to reduce owner-worker conflict and correct insufficient consumer purchasing power is to develop worker participation and profit-sharing schemes. In the long run, the solution is worker-owned businesses.

Argument 2: The profit system is inherently inefficient.

Profit is an unnecessary, extra cost piled on top of genuine production costs. As such, it is wasteful. If this waste were eliminated, prices would fall and everyone would be better off. As philosopher Ted Honderich has stated this case:

> If there are two ways of [producing] some valuable thing, and the second way involves not only the costs of [producing] it . . . but also [unnecessary] profits of millions or billions of dollars or pounds, then . . . the sec-

ond way is patently and tremendously less efficient.[33]

Argument 3: Quite apart from its injustice and inefficiency, the profit system does not give us the goods that we need.

Private businesses exist to make money. They must make money right now, or at least soon, not at some indefinite point in the future. Their focus is accordingly on immediate profit opportunities for the owners (that is, the few), not on the present and future needs of customers (that is, the many). In effect, there is a glaring conflict between "production for profit" and "production for people's use," and under our existing system "production for use" takes the hindmost. As history professor and popular commentator Howard Zinn explains this:

> The profit motive ... has ... distorted our whole economic and social system by making profit the key to what is produced and therefore leaving important things unproduced and stupid things produced [as well as] leaving some people rich and some people poor.[34]

Young European protestors against "global capitalism" have made the same point on their banners and placards: "People Not Profit."[35]

Argument 4: Even when the profit system produces the right goods, it denies them to those who need them the most, the poor.

This may be tolerable in some consumer areas, but not in areas of basic need such as healthcare. Cynthia Tucker, editorial page editor of *The Atlanta Journal–Constitution*, explains:

> The profit motive doesn't improve every enterprise.... [The] healthcare industry [currently] ... exist[s] to make money.... They jack up the prices ... and restrict ... [service] to those who can afford it.... [This] has gone too far.[36]

9

Are Private Profits Necessary?—Yes

Argument 5: Prices and profits work together as an indispensable signaling device.

THE DESIRE AND need, that is, the demand for particular products is constantly shifting. People choose this now, that later. Meanwhile the supply of products also shifts depending on an infinite number of variables (for example, weather affects the supply of crops). Information about both demand and supply is communicated to everyone by prices. Higher prices signal more demand or less supply, lower prices signal the opposite. This radically simplifies economic life.

As important as prices are for signaling conditions, they cannot do their work without profits. For example, assume that I am in the applesauce business and that profits are high because of heavy consumer demand or unusually low apple or sugar costs. The high profits give me the cash (or the credit) to step up my production. In addition other producers will likely do the same, and some new producers may be attracted into the business. In either case, supply will rise until profits fall back to more modest levels.

On the other hand, if profits fall far enough, supply will contract, so that output will again be brought into better balance with consumer demand. Everybody who wants applesauce will then get it, and producers will earn the profits necessary to keep recreating a balance. The key point to remember is that the quest for profits in a competitive market tends to increase supply, thereby lowering, not raising consumer prices. The quest for profits also drives competitors to work hard at lowering their costs. The dynamic of competition eventually translates lower costs into lower prices as well.

The profit system is especially good at identifying "chokepoints" or "bottlenecks" in the economic system, places where production is difficult or inefficient and where profit "tolls" are consequently high. For example, Mark Kurlansky in his book *Cod* has sketched the development of the huge cod-fishing industry since the sixteenth century, an industry that in earlier centuries furnished a high percentage of the total protein available to Europeans. At first the chokepoint was the ships, which were too small and flimsy. This attracted capital and better ship designs, so that the profit of ship owners eventually fell.

The next chokepoint was ports immediately adjacent to the fishing grounds, because the fish could not be kept long without processing, and nearby processors were able to charge high rates. As ships got faster, however, the small ports were bypassed, and the chokepoint moved to larger ports such as Boston. These larger ports were much more efficient than the smaller ones, but still commanded high prices and earned high profits. Finally, refrigerated container ships enabled fishing companies to bypass processing centers entirely.

Step by step, investment flowed to where the process was least efficient, where high profits signaled both a problem and an opportunity. In each case, the problems were solved, the chokepoint profits were reduced or eliminated through investment and competition, and consumers directly benefited from the increase in efficiency through steadily declining prices.[37] Although everyone benefited from this process, the poor benefited especially, because it meant that they could afford more protein in their diet.

Even Karl Marx, the father of Communism, acknowledged that the profit system reduces prices. He said as much in the *Communist Manifesto* of 1848:

> The cheap prices of its commodities are
> the heavy artillery with which [the profit
> system] . . . compels all nations, on pain of
> extinction, to adopt the [profit] mode of
> production.[38]

When the Soviet Union came into being during
World War One as the first Communist state, many
of its founders assumed that both prices and profits
would be abolished. This was complicated by Marx's
puzzling failure to suggest exactly how this might be
done. A decision was eventually reached to keep prices
and profits, although the latter would be "for all."

Economist Ludwig von Mises responded that a system of public prices and profits was impossible, that
only private prices and profits could provide the necessary information flow and calculations, and thus organize, direct, and grow an economy. Von Mises summarized the problem in this way:

> It is not enough to tell a man not to buy on
> the cheapest market and not to sell on the
> dearest market. . . . One must establish unam-
> biguous rules for the guidance of conduct in
> each concrete situation.[39]

Von Mises's thesis was violently disputed but never
successfully rebutted, either in theory or in practice.
The Soviet Union by the 1960s had from five to nine
price and profit systems according to varying accounts,
but none seemed to work.[40] As Oystein Dahle, a Nor-

wegian oil executive, has said, "Socialism collapsed because it did not allow prices to tell the economic truth."[41]

Not every equalitarian, to be sure, accepts the notion that free prices and profits are necessary as a signaling device. A letter writer to the Mises Institute, for example, argues that real "socialism" has yet to be tried:

> The Soviet Union was a system of capitalism run by the state. Nothing more, nothing less. . . . The alternative to a centrally planned capitalist economy or a laissez-faire capitalist economy is a decentralized moneyless marketless economy.[42]

The writer does not specify, but probably had in mind a series of independent, isolated economic communes.

Argument 6: Profits are also indispensable as a system of positive and negative incentives that, importantly, are objectively scored.

We usually think of the game of business being scored in profits, but it is even more importantly scored in losses and bankruptcies. As economist Wilhelm Ropke has written:

> Since the fear of loss appears to be of more moment than the desire for gain, it may be said that our economic system (in the final analysis) is regulated by bankruptcy.[43]

Economist Milton Friedman has similarly argued that the "profit" system should really be called the "profit and loss" system, that the "stick" is at least as important as the "carrot."

The carrot of profit and the stick of loss in general persuade us either to change or to accept change, something that people are more often than not reluctant to do. Economic growth by definition entails change; without it we would all still be hunting and gathering, or at least those few of us who could still survive within such a restricted economic environment. Yet many people are simply uncomfortable with change, others may be lazy, and vested interests will always fight hard against change if they can.

People can of course be motivated to change by other, more directly coercive methods. Stalin bent millions to his will through sheer terror. But, as a general rule, coercion is extremely inefficient, because people have a thousand ways of resisting, passively as well as actively. If one reads the memoirs of large slaveholders in the American South before the Civil War,[44] they are full of fretting about the incessant passive resistance of the slaves, even in the face of cruel punishments. That such an inefficient system survived at all can only be attributed to the boom prices being paid at the time for American cotton by English clothing manufacturers.

Argument 7: At first glance, it might seem that the profit system just produces what rich people want, not what the greater number of people need. But this is wrong.

The profit system is guided by profits, and the greatest profits are earned, not by catering to the wants and whims of the rich, but rather by meeting the genuine needs of large numbers of people. Economist Ludwig von Mises explains:

> Mass production ... [is] the fundamental principle of [profit-seeking] industry.... big business, the target of the most fanatic attacks by the so-called leftists, produces ... for the masses.[45]

Economist Milton Friedman elaborates this point further:

> Progress ... over the past century ... has freed the masses from backbreaking toil and has made available to them products and services that were formerly the monopoly of the upper classes.... [46] The rich in Ancient Greece would have ... welcomed the improvements in transportation and in medicine, but for the rest, the great achievements of [profit seeking] have redounded primarily to the benefit of the ordinary person.[47]

It is natural to feel that something is very amiss when the profit system stops making shoes before all the poor children have them. It is equally puzzling (and disturbing) when the profit system seems incapable of reducing healthcare prices, so that healthcare becomes more and more unaffordable for the poor. But if one looks closely at what is really happening, it will be apparent that profit-making is not to blame.

Nobody wants poor children to go without shoes. But we still operate in an environment of economic scarcity, which means that trade-offs must continually be made. If we keep making shoes, we will have more of them and each pair will be cheaper and cheaper. But then we will have to accept less of something else and higher costs for each unit of that. The only "waste" in the system that one can fairly point to is the portion of rich people's income that is spent on luxuries.

The problem of healthcare differs from the problem of insufficient shoes for poor children. The difference is that the healthcare industry has been socialized, fully in Britain and Canada, half (in terms of payment source) in the United States. Consequently, contrary to Cynthia Tucker, profit-making is only part of the equation, and mixing profit-based and government-led systems virtually guarantees failure.

The crux of the problem is that government has subsidized more and more healthcare costs. This has dramatically increased demand, but government has done nothing to increase supply. Indeed, government regulations and licensing restrict supply, keep it from growing. More demand, together with the same or less supply, leads to higher prices, then more subsidies, then still higher prices, in a vicious circle that particularly injures the poor, the aged, and the unemployed. Moreover, the high cost of healthcare also contributes to unemployment, because, (at least in the U.S.), employers often pay for health insurance, and rising health costs lead to less hiring. Healthcare costs were a particularly important factor in reducing payroll growth in the U.S. at the beginning of the twenty-first century.

Argument 8: It is also understandable that many people think of profits as "stolen" from workers.

After all, do not worker's wages come out of the "skin" of owners and vice versa? Is this not a classic example of a "zero-sum game"? Surprisingly, the answer is no.

A business divided will not stand. Owners and workers must cooperate if they are to survive and thrive and, in particular, to hold their own against competitors, who are surely the more meaningful antagonists. Furthermore, although pay raises and bonuses feel good, and could be taken out of profits in the short run, we have seen that profits are needed to pay for investment, either directly or by attracting investors. And it is precisely this stream of investment that provides workers with the tools, training, and other support necessary to make them more productive, which in turn justifies and pays for the raises or bonuses.

Running a successful business is always a balancing act. If wages are too low, workers will leave. If wages are too high, profits will be too low to pay for productivity-enhancing investments or other planned expansion. Workers should applaud productivity-enhancing investments, because studies show that, over time, they get all the return on such investments in the form of higher wages, or at least all the return that does not go to customers in the form of lower prices.

It is not surprising, on reflection, that over the years a business's profits and wages tend to rise or fall together, with profits leading a bit, or that this same pattern holds for the economy as a whole. Nor is it surprising that overall employment tends to follow profits, since businesses use profits to invest in workers as well as capital equipment. The only part of profits the workers in general do not directly benefit from is, again, business owners' luxury spending, and of course workers in luxury industries even benefit from that. On balance, a rise in genuine, sustainable profits is very good news for an economy, because it means that higher employment levels and wages are coming next.

Argument 9: Raising pay in one company will not increase the overall share of "labor."

Let us assume that a "widget" business is shortchanging its workers on pay and not even investing enough in the business to maintain its existing plant and equipment. This may be because the "widget" business is failing, and the profit-making system is forcing it to wind down and its employees to move on to better opportunities. If the business is not failing, it presumably will be failing soon, because in that case the owners' greed will cause it to lose its best workers and become less and less competitive.

But assume that the business is sound, is simply underpaying its workers, that the workers strike, that wages are substantially raised, and that the owners are compelled to stop being greedy. In this case, a blow has been struck for Labor and against Capital, has it not? Well, no. The answer is no because the workers will take their new wages and buy things with them. These new purchases will in turn swell the sales and profits of other business owners, so that economy wide profits will be unaffected, just as Labor and Capital aggregate shares will be unaffected.

In the meantime, the greedy owners may try to compensate for the higher wages they have been forced to pay by raising prices. This will probably backfire by reducing revenues and profits further. If not, it will raise "widget" prices for consumers who are also workers. This will particularly hurt workers who are retired or otherwise living off savings.[48] So it is impossible to say that the strike-won higher wages in the "widget" company represent a blow for Labor against Capital.

Argument 10: Employee business ownership creates as many problems as it solves.

Advocates of employee ownership or profit-sharing schemes see both as a way to create a better motivated

and thus more efficient workforce, a more just work-
place environment, and stronger consumer demand.[49]
At first glance, it might seem that no one could possibly oppose such a proposal. But, in reality, there are
important objections to it. In the first place, workers
are not an abstraction. They are individual human
beings who grow old and want to retire. What then?
Usually the retiring employees want to sell their shares
and profit from the sale, so they will sell to the highest bidder, which probably will not be other employees. If, alternatively, shares can only be sold to other
employees at modest prices, then the employees have
not been full equity owners. In addition, the restrictions on share transfer may make it impossible for the
firm to raise outside capital.

Most importantly, if employees owned the entire
economy, saving would plummet. As we have seen, it
is the special role of the rich to be forced to save and
invest—they alone have more than they can possibly
spend. Profit-sharing plans are also, unfortunately, subject to the same criticism: more often than not, they
represent a form of variable employee compensation,
not a true sharing of "profits." In true profit-sharing
plans, employees leave some (sometimes all) of their
"profits" in the business, just as outside owners do.

Argument 11: The kind of macroeconomics commonly taught in schools is misleading: it does not adequately acknowledge the role of profits.

Economist David Ricardo said in the early nineteenth century that "Nothing contributes so much to the prosperity and happiness of a country as high profits."[50]

Ricardo was right, and given the truth of what he said, one must wonder why modern macroeconomists have so little to say about profits. Macroeconomics texts are full of discussion about production growth, employment, inflation, etc., but profits are kept in the back room, generally out of sight. If profits are discussed, it is generally in the microeconomics section of a text, the part that concerns individual businesses and industries, not the economy as a whole.

10

Are Private Profits Necessary?—No/Yes

Argument 12: Profit-driven change is irrational and disorderly.

THE PROFIT-AND-LOSS SYSTEM, if unchecked, flies out of control. The carrots become too sweet, the sticks too hard, change becomes too rapid, too many people are displaced by it. No one knows where the change will take us, because it is rudderless and unguided, and may quickly plunge us into chaos or ruin.

Argument 13: Response.

A price-and-profit system gives us order, not chaos,

an order led and guided by the wishes of consumers. This is a spontaneous order,[51] like the common laws that have been developed through trials over the centuries, or rules of grammar or speech.

To think that order cannot exist without a leader's visible commands is natural, but it is untrue. As economist Friedrich Hayek has written:

> This is not a dispute about whether planning is to be done or not. It is a dispute as to whether planning is to be done centrally, by one authority for the whole economic system, or is to be divided among many individuals.[52]

We can certainly install a more visible central command, restrict the carrots that seem too sweet, soften the sticks, slow or better regulate the rate of change, but we will get more chaos, not less, and more economic corruption and poverty to boot.

Argument 14: The pot-of-gold-at-the-end-of-the-rainbow atmosphere of the profit system, with its uncertain, excessive, and largely undeserved rewards, encourages business owners to adopt a short-term, grab-it-and-flee mentality.

The right kind of economic system should encourage people to regard work as its own reward, to appreciate the joys of serving others, and to approach work with patience and perseverance. The idea of chasing a big pay-off is inimical to all these ideals.

Argument 15: Response.

The profit system is not a treasure hunt and does not encourage short-termism. Most new businesses lose money for a time; entrepreneurs must have faith, patience, and the judgment to know when they are failing and when they are simply suffering the usual setbacks in starting something new.

If profit-seekers have patience, and also the gift of good judgment, they will eventually earn profits, and the profits will start to compound. At first this is a glacially slow process. If $10,000 in starting capital, or in initial profits, grows each year by 12%, it will take twenty years to pass $100,000. But, if the growth rate is maintained, the law of large numbers takes over, and in twenty more years the number will reach $1,000,000. If the $1,000,000 keeps doubling every six years, it will become a fantastic figure, as described in chapter one. Such a system can hardly be said to encourage short-termism.

What the profit system does encourage, apart from patience, is to keep growing, keep compounding, no matter how low the rate of annual increase. Britain became the leading economic power, the wonder and envy of the world, all based on an estimated compound economic growth rate of barely 2% a year from 1780 to 1914.[53] Two percent may not sound impressive to us, but it was far higher than any nation had ever achieved, especially over long periods.

Argument 16: Economic growth requires cooperation. The profit system encourages cutthroat, dog-eat-dog competition, which is the opposite of cooperation.

How can anyone imagine that setting one person against another will encourage cooperation? This defies logic. If we want more cooperation, and we should, we must teach a cooperative ethic, and create economic institutions that support this ethic.

Argument 17: Response.

Profit-seeking economic competition is not anti-cooperative. Nor is it usually cutthroat or dog-eat-dog. It is true that competition channels aggressive tendencies into socially useful purposes, in sharp contrast to warfare or pillage. But business competition in general takes place within a cooperative framework, similar to organized sports such as the Olympics.

Much business competition is not even personal, unlike sports. Economist Milton Friedman has pointed out that wheat farmers tend to view each other as colleagues, because no one wheat farmer's output or actions has much direct impact on another. But strictly speaking, they are economic competitors. Truly ruthless competition is to be found in politics which, unlike business, truly is a zero-sum game, and in any case ruthlessness can be found in any human occupation, including teaching, social services, or religion.

Argument 18: We can and should devise a better economic system, one that appeals to our higher, not our lower nature.

Whatever problems may arise with employee ownership, they can be overcome with a cooperative and innovative spirit. For example, actual ownership might reside not in specific employees, but in a trust for the benefit of employees. Such a trust could be allowed to sell shares to outsiders to raise business capital, but not to "cash out" employee owners. State ownership of the economy has not generally worked well, but true employee ownership has not yet been tried and holds immense promise. In general, the profit system should be a transitional form of human economic organization, one that we can eventually outgrow and put behind us.

Part Five

Profit-making
and Depressions

11

Does the Profit System Cause Depressions?— Yes/No

Argument 1: The blind selfishness of profit-driven markets is incompatible with employment stability.

JOURNALIST AND PHILOSOPHER Walter Lippmann stated this case clearly during the Great Depression: "An uncoordinated, unplanned, disorderly individualism . . . inevitably produces alternating periods of boom and depression."[54]

A *Washington Post* editorial writer echoed Lippmann over sixty years later: "Markets, following their own blind logic, typically overreact and, left to their own impulses, can do great damage."[55] Investor, speculator, and philosopher George Soros warned that:

> There is [an erroneous] belief that markets are self correcting. . . . To put the matter simply, market forces, if they are given complete authority even in the purely economic and financial arenas, produce chaos and could ultimately lead to the downfall of the global [economic] system.[56]

It follows from this viewpoint that "[One of] the most important function[s] for . . . government . . . is ensuring macroeconomic stability."[57]

Lippmann explained how to go about it:

> The state [should] undertake . . . to counteract the mass errors of the individualist crowd by doing the opposite of what the crowd is doing; it saves when the crowd is spending too much; it borrows when the crowd is saving too much; it economizes when the crowd is extravagant, and it spends when the crowd is afraid to spend. . . . [This] compensatory method is, I believe, an epoch-making invention.[58]

Argument 2: Response.

As explained earlier, profit-driven markets are the opposite of disorderly. They are, in fact, the best way to organize ourselves, and are continually led and guided by the wishes of consumers.

The idea that government can in some way "compensate" for market "errors" has proven to be not "an epoch-making invention," but rather a tragic delusion. Politicians are even less likely than consumers to restrain themselves during a boom. They want to spend more, not less, deceiving themselves that the boom will last forever. Their recklessness, more than any other factor, tips the boom into bust.

Argument 3: Profit-driven economies are inherently prone to depression.

This is because business owners try to keep wages as low as possible, assuming that this will fatten profits. What is forgotten is that workers are also consumers. Underpaid consumers will not be able to buy all the goods produced.

Walter Lippmann believed that this was the fundamental cause of the Great Depression of the 1930s: "The heart of the problem . . . [has been] . . . an insufficiency of consumer . . . purchasing power." [59]

Argument 4: Response

The "employee/consumer purchasing power theory" articulated in Argument 3 is false. It is false because a business owner who underpays employees will take the gains and either reinvest them in the economy, to be earned by other workers, or buy luxury goods, which must also be produced by other workers, or pay dividends to other shareholders, who will also either invest or buy. So long as the money is circulating in this way, there should be no failure or crisis of demand.

What really upsets the system are not low wages per se, but an imbalance among wages, prices, profits, and investment. The right balance of these variables helps workers the most, both in their roles as workers and as consumers. In retrospect, it is tragic that the fallacies of the "employee purchasing power theory" guided (actually misguided) the actions of both the Hoover and Roosevelt administrations during the Great Depression of the 1930s.

Argument 5: To achieve employment stability, we need stable prices in our economy. The profit system gives us erratic prices, occasionally stable, more often rising (inflation) or falling (deflation). Falling prices in particular are a primary cause of depressions.

When we order flour or sugar, we expect to get a specified weight in pounds or kilograms. When we travel from city to city, we also know that we can rely on standard units of measurement, whether miles or kilometers. Imagine, now, that pounds, kilograms, miles, and kilometers all fluctuated in value from day to day. Economic chaos would ensue.

If we do not accept fluctuating weights and distances, why should we accept fluctuating money values? Not knowing what a dollar or euro will be worth tomorrow, expressed against each other, or even more importantly expressed as an underlying basket of goods that each will buy, is confusing, disorienting, and destabilizing.

If I am saving for my retirement in twenty years, it would greatly simplify life to know that a dollar would buy as much then as now. If I am a home-builder and have built a home without a contracted buyer, all my work may be in vain if prices fall just when I am ready to sell. And if I have borrowed a lot of money, and have to pay it back in money that has risen in value (money rises in value as prices fall), I could be utterly ruined. None of this is hypothetical. Prices did fall at the onset of the Great Depression, millions of businesses and especially debtors were forced into bankruptcy, and massive unemployment resulted.

Unfortunately, a profit system virtually guarantees that prices will fall. In the first place, the market system, as we have previously seen, invests its capital in productivity-enhancing equipment in order to reduce costs. Even if the business owner's goal is to reduce costs without reducing prices, competition soon drives prices down with costs.

In the second place, business owners get carried away and overproduce, so that prices may start to free fall. Business confidence will then collapse with prices, and what is called a "debt deflationary downward spiral" will drag even strong businesses and individuals down with it. Falling prices are just exceptionally dangerous for an economy, and should not be tolerated.

Argument 6: Response.

Prices have nothing in common with weights and distances. Nor should we want them to be stable. On the contrary, we should want them to fall.

The very purpose of free markets is to reduce prices so that more and more people can afford to buy the goods and services being produced. Many products arrive as luxury goods, far too expensive for the average person to own, but are eventually mass produced at reasonable prices for everyone. Automobiles and computers are particularly dramatic instances of this. Why should we try to thwart this process by keeping economy-wide prices artificially high, especially when falling prices will do more than anything to help the poor? Wanting lower prices is just common sense. Opposing them is an example of twisted logic, of theoretical economics run amok.

The objective here is, of course, steadily and gently falling prices, not a precipitate collapse, leading to a downward spiral of failing businesses. But if debt deflation does come, better for government to stand back and let the market sort itself out.

Wages in particular should be allowed to fall with prices. This need not hurt workers, because lower wages can buy the same consumer basket as before if prices are lower. Once the market has sorted out the right relationship among prices, wages, and other costs, profits, and employment levels will bounce back and good economic times will return.

In all this, it is important to remember that free markets are so efficient because they offer people an opportunity not just to make money, but also to lose it. Once ideas, investments, businesses prove to be failures, they should be weeded out as quickly and unequivocally as possible.

Before the 1930s, and the advent of an activist government, there were depressions to be sure, but they were brief. As economist Friedrich Hayek said in an interview toward the end of his life, "My great example is ... the U.S. in 1921 and 1922[.] After six months of depression, prices came down by 44%. Then the economy started off on another boom."[60]

This was in sharp contrast to the Great Depression of the thirties, when falling prices were combated and wages kept artificially high by both the Hoover and Roosevelt administrations. As a direct result, unemployment kept deepening and depression lingered on amidst terrible human suffering.

Nor are economic safety nets a good idea. When speculators are bailed out from their soured speculations, they will simply speculate more. When no serious consequences follow from reckless debts or gambling, recklessness and gambling will increase exponentially. This problem of "moral hazard" confronts us whether we are dealing with countries, companies, or individuals. The lesson to be learned, in economist Wilhelm Ropke's words, is that "The more [government] stabilization, the less stability."[61]

Argument 7: Response.

If sharp falls in prices could be matched by sharp falls in wages, then, yes, markets might be able to pull themselves out of depressions on their own. But this is completely unrealistic. Modern workers will not, under any circumstances, accept lower wages. If prices fall dramatically, wages will not fall, profits will collapse, massive unemployment will follow, and depression will persist indefinitely.

The only way to get out of this predicament is for government to intervene and pump additional money into the economy. If the amount of goods and services remains the same, but the amount of money in circulation dramatically increases, the prices of goods and services should rise.

To see why this is so, imagine yourself on a desert island with one companion, one dollar, two apples, and nothing else. The price of each apple would logically be 50¢. But if another dollar landed on the beach inside a bottle, the price per apple would logically rise to $1.

How does government get additional money into the economy? It might borrow it from individuals and businesses and then spend it. But this is only effective if the private parties are keeping their money under a mattress, out of circulation.

Most likely, government will also need to "print" new money. This new money is made available to banks, which lend it in the ordinary way, thereby moving it out into the economy.*

Can it really be this simple to cure or even better to avoid deflation and thus avoid economic slumps? Economist Paul Krugman, a leading advocate of active monetary interventions, acknowledges that

> To many people it seems obvious that massive economic slumps must have deep roots. To them, [the] argument that they . . . can be cured by [the government] printing a bit more money seems unbelievable.[62]

But he assures us that deflation (and depression) can indeed be cured or avoided through the simple expedient of expanding the amount of money in circulation whenever prices are falling or seem in danger of falling.

Argument 8: Response.

When government "prints" new money and makes it available to banks to lend out, there may or may not be borrowers to take it. If people are sufficiently frightened, they will try to repay loans rather than take out new ones. In this case, the government may have to spend the money itself to get it into the economy and thereby boost prices.

---

* For a more technical description of how this is done, see this book's companion volume, *How Much Money Does An Economy Need?*, forthcoming from Axios Press in January 2008.

If banks are able to lend the new money, no one can be sure where it will go. Businesses that desperately need a price increase may not benefit from the new money that is circulating while businesses with fat profit margins may benefit instead. Monetary intervention is a crude and uncertain tool at best.

More seriously, there is something perverse about using "easy" money to correct a debt deflation. After all, it is usually "easy" money that lures people into taking on excessive debt in the first place during the boom phase, before the inevitability of the bust becomes apparent.

As economist Friedrich Hayek said in the 1930s:

> To combat the depression by [printing more money and encouraging more debt] is to attempt to cure the evil by the very means which brought it about.[63]

In effect, trying to cure an economic slump caused by easy money with even easier money is like trying to cure a hangover with more alcohol. And if this policy is combined, as it often is, with tighter and tighter business regulation and an abandonment of free trade in favor of protectionism, the effects can be particularly disastrous.

Quite apart from the perverseness of active monetary intervention, there are other reasons to be suspicious of it. For one thing, why is it done in such a stealthy, indeed in such a clandestine manner? The straightforward way for government to print money is to run it off printing presses. This is what governments used to do. But now, instead, they first borrow money from private parties, especially banks, by selling bonds to the banks, then buy in the same bonds through their central banks. Since the central bank checks used for this purpose are drawn out of thin air, the effect is identical to printing money outright, but concealed from the eyes of all but a few experts.

One reason that governments prefer to "print" new money stealthily is that "printing" new money is really a form of taxation, albeit an indirect and thus more easily concealable form. A bit of math will illustrate why this is so. Assume that an economy consists of one dollar and various goods and services. The government can either take 25¢ in tax revenue or "print" 33.3¢ for its own use. Either way, the authorities now command 25% of all goods and services (25¢ is a quarter of $1.00 and 33.3¢ is a quarter of $1.00 plus 33.3¢). Because the government now commands 25% of all goods and services, private individuals have 25% less, although they will generally be much more aware of the change when directly taxed.

Part Six

The Global
Profit System

12

Does Global Free Trade*
Destroy Jobs?—Yes

Argument 1: Free trade destroys jobs, especially good, high-paying jobs.

AWRENCE SUMMERS, FORMER World Bank chief economist, U.S. secretary of the treasury, and president of Harvard University, has summarized the case against free trade as follows:

---

* "Free" trade may be defined as the opposite of "protectionism" or "managed" trade. Protectionism or "managed" trade generally consists of: tariffs (taxes on imports); non-tariff barriers (regulations that inhibit imports); quotas (direct limits on imports); restrictive trade rules (e.g., "anti-dumping" laws that demand minimum prices for imports); or asset purchase restrictions (e.g., forbidding foreign majority ownership of domestic industries).

> Abe Lincoln captured the basic intuition of almost anyone ... when he said that ... if he bought a coat from an American, he had a coat and an American had a dollar, and that ... it seemed to him better to do it ... [that] way.[64]

Summers went on to say that he disagrees with Lincoln's point of view, as indeed a majority of economists do. But Jerry Flint, a *Forbes* automobile-industry columnist, has his own response to that:

> You can't help noticing that the folks supporting free trade never have their jobs threatened: editorial writers, economists, professors. . . . Imagine colleges replacing those two-classes-a-week professors with brainiacs from India at $50 a class.[65]

Peter Lynch, a legendary American investment fund manager, has also been skeptical about finding jobs in a free-trading global marketplace:

> We keep showing more workers, but they're all making [low wages]. . . . It seems to me that if you give a dollar more to the consumer and he buys a Japanese-produced Toyota with it, you don't help the U.S. economy much. . . . [Other nations are] doing [to the U.S.] what [John D.] Rockefeller [Sr.] did. . . . They dump a product, they drive everybody out. . . . It's totally unfair trade.[66]

Argument 2: Left to itself, unrestrained free world trade produces a "race to the bottom" for labor and environmental standards.

The central flaw of a free market, whether domestic or global, is its underlying ideology of greed. Profit becomes the be-all and end-all of existence; human decency be damned. The result is not just cutthroat competition and rampant product "dumping," but labor, social, and environmental "dumping" as well. In effect, to attract global capital, governments everywhere dismantle safeguards against child labor, unbearable working conditions, inhumane wages, and pollution. As William Greider has written:

> Finance capital . . . is . . . the Robespierre . . . of this [global capitalist] revolution . . . collectively act[ing] . . . like a Committee of Public Safety presiding over the Terror.[67]

Al Sharpton, preacher and 2004 candidate for the Democratic nomination for U.S. president, adds that

> We cannot [allow a] trade policy that overlooks labor, overlooks workers' rights, overlooks environmental concerns. . . . African-Americans are here [in the U.S. because of] . . . bad trade policy.[68]

Some critics of global capitalism hope to tame it, to negotiate global regulations ensuring decent working and environmental standards. But these hopes are naive at best. Historian Arthur Schlesinger, Jr. understands what is really happening, and how helpless nation states are to rein in world markets:

> The computer turns the untrammeled market into a global juggernaut crashing across frontiers, enfeebling national powers of taxation and regulation, undercutting national management of interest rates and exchange rates, widening disparities of wealth both within and between nations, dragging down labor standards, degrading the environment."[69]

Argument 3: Free trade is ultimately about exploitation.

No one should be under any illusion that the billions of dollars of investment poured into the developing world are intended as a charitable act. The money is intended to create an abject dependency, and rarely fails to achieve this end. Richard Gephardt, candidate for the Democratic nomination for U.S. president in 2004, courageously noted the "raw human exploitation for the profit of a few corporations"[70] in global trade. Some headlines in Roman Catholic publications have also captured the real story:

- ■■ "Nearly 1 Billion Starve while Markets Boom" (*National Catholic Reporter*)
- ■■ "Making Profit the World's Highest Law" (*National Catholic Reporter*)

- ■■ "A New Imperialism" (*Commonweal*)
- ■■ "Global Village or Global Pillage?" (*Commonweal*)
- ■■ "Who Pays the Price for Trade: Farmers, Workers, and the Unemployed" (*Commonweal*)

Activists around the world are committed to fighting the inhuman values of global capitalism and regularly turn out to protest at meetings of the World Bank, the International Monetary Fund, or the World Trade Organization, institutions supposed to facilitate world trade. One such activist, Jaggi Singh, explains that his activism is

> About changing the world, creating structures, frameworks, institutions, communities, neighborhoods that are based on our values, which are values of social justice, mutual aid, solidarity, and direct democracy.[71]

13

Does Global Free Trade Destroy Jobs?—No

Argument 4: Free trade produces more and better jobs.

THE PRESERVATION OR protection of jobs is a dead-end policy. As noted previously, if everyone had preserved and protected their jobs from the stone age on, we would all be hunting and gathering. We have escaped that fate by learning to innovate, to specialize, and, in global trade, to pursue our comparative advantage.

The phrase "comparative advantage" is often misunderstood. It does not mean that a country should find something that it can produce more cheaply than other countries and specialize in that. If a country can produce something more cheaply than any other country, that is called an "'absolute advantage," not a comparative advantage.

Comparative advantage refers to what a country does best, without regard to whether there is an absolute advantage. The basic idea, sketched by Adam Smith in the eighteenth century, and formulated more precisely a few decades later by David Ricardo, is that a country, like an individual, should concentrate on what it does best, and then trade with other countries to obtain what others do best. Even if (hypothetically) one country has an absolute advantage in everything and another country has an absolute advantage in nothing, the two countries will be well-advised to divide up the tasks and exchange their work.

In his book *Basic Economics*, Thomas Sowell provides a good example of this. He asks us to assume, for purpose of illustration, that the United States makes both shirts and shoes more cheaply than Canada. In other words, the U.S. has an absolute advantage in both articles. Specifically, the U.S. makes shirts more than twice as cheaply and shoes 25% more cheaply. Based on these numbers, one might conclude that the U.S. should continue making shirts and shoes for itself, but this would be incorrect. Since the U.S. is much more cost effective in shirts, relatively speaking, than it is in shoes, it will still pay to concentrate on shirts and leave the shoes to Canada. If the U.S. and Canada team up in this way, the total production of shirts and shoes mathematically increases by about 20% and 11% respectively. Just by specializing and trading, the two countries in this hypothetical example become measurably richer.[72]

Comparative advantage also tells us that when we buy a cheaper foreign import we may be helping to put a fellow countryman out of a job, but we are also helping another fellow countryman, probably more than one fellow countryman, to find a job.

Assume, for example, that we live in a completely closed economy without foreign trade. The ban on foreign trade lifts and many adjustments are necessary. If our domestic steel manufacturers are selling their product at higher than the world price, they will have to reduce prices and probably lay off workers. Many of our other companies, however, are steel users, not steel sellers. The math of comparative advantage suggests that they will gain more from the lower steel prices than the sellers will lose. The converse is also true: if steel prices before opening to world trade are lower than the world price, the steel companies will gain. And they will gain more than domestic steel users will lose, so that employment will also increase in this case.

Assuming that it is the steel users who gain, and the steel workers who lose, there will be a tendency for the public to see only the unemployed steel workers, not the newly employed auto or other workers. Voters may then listen to steel industry blandishments that steel tariffs are needed to save steel jobs without realizing that the net effect of tariffs would be to reduce, not increase, overall employment. The bottom line is that people cannot be in two places at once. By allowing cheaper foreign imports to come in, workers can be placed in more productive, and therefore better paying, jobs.

These principles are well established for the import or export of goods. It is not as widely recognized that they are just as relevant for the "outsourcing" of service jobs over the internet or telephone lines. The savings achieved by importing electronic services has enabled many companies to prosper, where they otherwise might have stagnated or failed, and thus to hire more employees rather than fewer.[73]

As a general rule, if we are going to specialize, and then exchange the fruit of our specialized labor, it helps to broaden the circle of shared labor, not restrict it. The United States is a good example of this. It represents the largest free-trade zone in the world, as measured by the volume of goods and services exchanged. In fact, the volume of trade inside the U.S. may be as large as the total volume of global trade among countries.

Within the U.S., at the present time, approximately one in twenty jobs disappears each year.[74] This in turn makes it possible for the economy to keep changing and growing. Indeed, the most economically thriving U.S. regions tend to have the greatest job loss, but also the greatest job creation. Job turnover can be hard on employees, especially older ones, but it is essential for job growth, economic growth, and an improving standard of living.

Whatever its critics say, the math of comparative advantage still works. Sharing the work of the world makes everyone richer, even the already rich nations. It is true that, on a purely relative basis, the developing nations should make bigger strides. In effect, all nations should benefit, but the gap between rich and poor should close, because the poor should grow faster. The already rich may then feel poorer, because the income gap has shrunk and there is more competition for the most prized consumer goods and collectibles. But, subjective feelings aside, there is no reason why the already rich should lose wealth, or why comparative advantage will suddenly produce winners and losers rather than mutual winners.

The protection of existing jobs through trade barriers is a formula for impoverishment under any circumstances. But, as Llewellyn Rockwell, the president of the Ludwig von Mises Institute, has noted:

> The tragedy of [government trade restriction and protectionism] is that it tends to creep up when it can do the most damage, that is, during economic downturns.[75]

The one thousand economists who argued against the Smoot–Hawley Tariff Act, which imposed stiff new taxes on goods coming into the United States just as the country was falling into the Great Depression, would presumably agree.

Argument 5: Global markets are not trashing labor and environmental standards.

Economist Jagdish Bhagwati replies to this charge:

■■ "Lower [labor and environmental] standards may ... repel, instead of attract [Direct Fixed Investment from abroad].[76]

■■ "Several empirical studies ... find that multinationals pay what economists now call a 'wage premium' ... [of about] 10 percent. ... Affiliates of U.S. multinationals sometimes pay ... a premium that ranges from 40 to 100 percent."[77]

■■ "Demands (for enforcement of more uniform global standards) ... [often reflect a] desire to raise the costs of production of rivals abroad. ...[78] Anti-dumping processes have become the favoured tool of protectionists today. Their extension to eco-dumping (and equally to social-dumping) ... will lead ... to ... more [of] ... the same."[79]

Argument 6: Global free trade is not at all about exploitation.

Global free markets are not a new form of imperialism launched to oppress and exploit the poor. These ideas, which originated with Marxist-Leninist Communism, should have perished with it.

It is perfectly true that global markets make the life of the rich more prosperous and comfortable. Lord Keynes described the pleasures of the first global economy, the one that was shattered by World War One. It enabled the wealthy and even the not-so-wealthy

> Inhabitant of London . . . [to] order by telephone, sipping his morning tea in bed, the various products of the whole earth, in such quantity as he might see fit, and reasonably expect their early delivery upon his doorstep; he could at the same moment and by the same means adventure his wealth in the natural resources and new enterprises of any quarter of the world, and share, without exertion or even trouble, in their prospective fruits and advantages; or he could decide to couple the security of his fortunes with the good faith of the townspeople of any substantial municipality in any continent that fancy or information might recommend. He could secure forthwith, if he wished it, cheap and comfortable means of transit to any country or climate without passport or other formality, could dispatch his servant into the neighboring office of a bank for such supply of precious metals as might seem convenient, and could then proceed abroad to foreign quar-

ters, without knowledge of their religion, language, or customs, bearing coined wealth upon his person, and would consider himself greatly aggrieved and much surprised at the least interference.[80]

Now by contrast consider what it is to be poor. A poor person may have some assets, even if only a farm animal. But the farm animal cannot be sent halfway around the world to fetch the best price. It must be sold locally at whatever price and on whatever terms are available. If the poor wish to buy something that might make them more productive, they are similarly constrained. The object can only be bought locally, usually at a high price, and this applies to the American slum dweller as well as to the poor and isolated Asian farmer.

If the poor do buy imported goods, the things they need will probably have a higher tariff attached to them than the luxury goods intended for the rich. This is true in almost every country. For example, a study by the Progressive Policy Institute in the U.S. showed that imported goods bought by poor or middle class people (e.g., clothes and shoes) had an average tariff of 10.5% versus an average tariff of only 0.8% on luxury goods.[81] Tariffs are not only a tax, albeit a hidden tax; they are a peculiarly regressive tax.

Proponents of trade-as-exploitation tend to regard foreign aid and multilateral loans as a kind of reparations for the damage done to the poor by greedy global capitalists. Viewed in this light, trade should be restricted and foreign aid vastly increased. But listen to Harvard historian Niall Ferguson:

> The authors of ... one recent study of 30 sub-Saharan African countries conclude ... that ... roughly 80 cents on every dollar borrowed by African countries flowed back [to the West] as capital flight in the same year. A similar story can be told for aid payments, a large proportion of which are simply stolen.[82]

The bottom line is that global free markets are imperfect, because people are imperfect, but they offer the best hope for the poor. Even economist Paul Krugman, a vocal critic of the profit system and especially the people who run it thinks so:

> [Opponents of global trade], whatever their intentions, are doing their best to make the poor even poorer.[83]

To which columnist David Brooks adds:

> Just once, I'd like to see [rock star] Bruce Springsteen stand up at a concert and speak the truth.... If you really want to reduce world poverty, you should be cheering on those ... investors jetting around the world.[84]

Part Seven

Glaring Inequality

14

Are There Alternatives to the Profit System? —Yes/No

Argument 1: Putting aside purely economic considerations, living with others on a share-and-share-alike basis is simply a better way to live.

THE PROPOSAL HERE is not one of state control of the economy. That was attempted in Russia and elsewhere during the twentieth century and was not a success.

The proposal is rather one of decentralization; of small scale rather than large scale; of many warm, sharing human communities rather than a single collectivity.

There are examples from the past as well as the present to draw upon for a smaller, more human-scaled equalitarianism. An economic textbook describes the Zuni people of the American Southwest during the 1920s as one model to follow:

> The family . . . comprising as many as twenty-five persons . . . was the main organizational unit of . . . economic life. Houses and land were privately owned, with the title being held by the women of the family. . . . In sharp contrast to the American economy, there was a general absence of acquisitiveness and competition. While there was no sale of goods and property at fixed market prices, there was an organized transfer of goods and services that took place within the framework of the tribe. To some extent, these transfers equalized the levels of living among the families of the tribe, preventing the extremes of poverty and great wealth.[85]

The Israeli kibbutz represents an even more intentional model of shared living, since kibbutz members join voluntarily and share everything as completely as possible on principle. In the early days before the formation of the State of Israel, this shared life was very hard. Malaria and dysentery had to be overcome, along with the harshest privations: cloth sacks stitched together for clothing, primitive communal privies, endless manual labor, three glasses to be shared by an entire community, as described by Prime Minister Golda Meir in her memoirs. Today the harshness is gone, but the ideal of a shared life remains.

An important manual of small-scale equalitarianism in Britain, America, India, and elsewhere is economist E. F. Schumacher's inspiring little book *Small is Beautiful*. Schumacher was a sensible, practical man who felt that people should simplify and downscale their life wherever possible without indulging in grandiose or utopian fantasies. He recognized that the greatest obstacle to human peace and happiness was not institutional arrangements per se, but the "greed, envy, hate, and lust"[86] within all of us. But he did think that large disparities of wealth inflamed both greed and envy, and he warned about the violence that rampant consumerism does to our soul:

> I suggest that the foundations of peace cannot be laid by universal prosperity, in the modern sense, because such prosperity, if attainable at all, is attainable only by cultivating ... drives ... which destroy intelligence, happiness, serenity, and thereby the peacefulness of man.[87]

The director of the E. F. Schumacher Society, Satish Kumar, a former monk, adds that:

> We are realizing, after 200 years of indus-

trial revolution, that we have gone too far in one direction. We need to bring some kind of balance between the spiritual and the material.[88]

Spirituality, peacefulness, even pacifism are ever-present threads in the fabric of contemporary small-scale equalitarianism. President Luiz Inacio ("Lula") da Silva of Brazil spoke for most equalitarians when he told a meeting of the Socialist International in 2003 that "The only war we should be waging is against hunger and inequality. That's a war worth fighting."[89]

And 2004 U. S. Democratic Party presidential primary candidate Dennis Kucinich made a similar point by proposing the creation of a federal "Department of Peace, which would seek to make non-violence an organizing principle in our society and to work with the nations of the world to make war itself archaic."[90]

In addition to spirituality, non-materialism, and peacefulness, ecology and environmental protection have also emerged as important themes of most small-scale equalitarian thinking. Thus the website of Twin Oaks, an intentional community of about eighty people near Charlottesville, Virginia, states that

Since the community's beginning in 1967, our way of life has reflected our values of cooperation, sharing, nonviolence, equality, and ecology.

All of this is in the most marked contrast to the old,

Marxist, large-scale equalitarian ideology of the past, which specifically attacked spirituality and non-materialism, rationalized violence and aggression, and left the most horrendous environmental depredations.

Argument 2: Response.

Small-scale equalitarianism is a vast improvement over the large-scale, state-run alternative. Indeed, large-scale equalitarianism is really a contradiction in terms. If sharing is statewide, it must be enforced. To be enforced, some individuals must be entrusted with police powers. If some people have police powers and others do not, how is that equal? It is simply an inequality of power rather than of money, and will soon mutate into an inequality of money as well, as it did in Communist Russia.

This is why the French Revolutionary slogan "liberty, equality, fraternity" is nonsensical. Liberty and equality are logical opposites. If people have liberty, they will become unequal. Even if government denies liberty to safeguard equality, equality will not last.

Small-scale equalitarianism is not illogical in the way that large-scale, state-run equalitarianism is. But there are reasons to doubt its practicality. The ancient Greek philosopher Aristotle pointed out that a share-and-share-alike approach to cooperation generally leads to conflict, because members of the group will not all work as hard, or will have sincere differences about the balance of work and leisure, either of which may lead to quarrels. From this point of view, an approach to cooperation that emphasizes independence, self-reliance, and reciprocal exchange will ultimately produce more friendship and mutual assistance.

In addition, if people are going to be quarrelsome about work or possessions, it is surely better to channel this aggression into prescribed forms of mutual exchange-based competition. As Samuel Johnson said, "There are few ways in which a man can be more innocently employed than in getting money."[91]

John Maynard Keynes made the same point:

> Dangerous human proclivities can be canalized into comparatively harmless channels by the opportunities for money-making and private wealth, which, if they cannot be satisfied in this way, may find their outlet in cruelty, the reckless pursuit of personal power and authority, and other forms of self-aggrandizement. It is better that a man should tyrannize over his bank balance than over his fellow-citizens.[92]

Opponents of equalitarianism generally take a "harder" rather than a "softer" line on a given social subject, and thus regard the small-scale equalitarian faith in Gandhian non-violence as a hopelessly utopian path to world peace. For example, here's what Joseph Alsop, leading political columnist after World War Two and an individual thoroughly grounded in ideals of independence and self-reliance, thought about the idea of unilateral disarmament or even military weakness:

> What do we need in America to endure? It isn't enough to say that we are very numerous, or that we are vastly rich in proportion to everyone else in the world. Being that rich simply makes us a target, if you think about it. Everybody else would like to divide up our goods. They'd like to chew us up like a dead whale on a beach, if we'd let them do it. And I have the warmest sympathy for that desire. It is perfectly understandable, and we mustn't complain about it.[93]

15

Should We Accept This Degree of Inequality?—No/Yes

Argument 3: Income inequality is unjust and uncharitable. No one should accept it with a clear conscience. The sooner and the closer we can get to equality the better.

MERICAN SOCIALIST MICHAEL Harrington believed that "[the profit system] . . . is outrageously unjust; it requires a continuing maldistribution of wealth in order to exist."[94]

David Gergen, advisor to American presidents from Nixon to Clinton, agrees that "a society where winners take all and losers take the hindmost is one that . . . [is] morally blind."[95]

The evidence for injustice lies on both sides of the vast income gap. On the one hand, billions of people desperately lack money for the barest necessities. On the other hand, a lucky individual will be fêted and showered with money just because he can dribble or throw a ball a bit better than others, or because he or she was born to rich parents. Between the extremes, we have dedicated and talented teachers and social workers who are woefully, even scandalously underpaid.

This system, as John Maynard Keynes said, is both "arbitrary and inequitable." Even if some degree of inequality is desirable for motivational purposes, as Keynes further observed: "Much lower stakes will serve the purpose equally well."[96]

The winners under this system should ask themselves: do I really deserve to have all this when others have so little? And, have I really "earned" it? Even if I have worked hard and made prudent choices, how far would I have gotten without the support of others? How remunerative would a sports talent be if there were not sports entertainment networks, or a talent for business without corporate legal protections and other assistance from government? Does anyone earn anything on his or her own? Is it not self-evident that each of us owes a great debt to others, and that this debt can best be paid by sharing more and by ensuring more equal outcomes? Is any other position truly moral?

None of us feels entirely comfortable when we confront a beggar or a homeless person on the street or see children living in abject poverty. We should heed our consciences, listen to what they are telling us. As Michael Harrington said about poverty statistics:

> These statistics represent an enormous, an unconscionable amount of human suffering in this land. They should be read with a sense of outrage.

> For until these facts shame us, until they stir us to action, the other America will continue to exist, a monstrous example of needless suffering in the most advanced society in the world.[97]

Argument 4: Response.

Our personal incomes are in no sense arbitrary. They are determined by supply and demand. Supply and demand tell us, in unequivocal terms, how useful we are in the eyes of others. Norman Van Cott explains:

> Our incomes—be they large, small or somewhere in between—reflect (1) our usefulness to our fellow citizens and (2) the ease with which fellow citizens can find substitutes for us.[98]

We may not want to hear the market's message. But the market does not discriminate. Only people discriminate. Employers who do so become less efficient, lose good employees or customers, suffer higher costs, and thus pay a penalty of lower profits. Over time, markets eradicate discrimination by persuading bigoted employers that they cannot afford to indulge their prejudices.

We may understandably object that markets treat people too much like commodities. But our labor (as distinct from ourselves) is a commodity, and is priced by consumers in exactly the same understandable and consistent way that other commodities are priced. There is nothing inequitable about this.

It may be objected that our financial success depends, not simply on effort or merit, but to a large extent on luck. If so, we are not lucky or unlucky in money alone. We are all lucky to become fetuses, since the odds are infinitesimal that any particular two gene pools will ever merge, we are lucky to be born, and lucky to reach maturity. From there we are lucky or unlucky in the genes we get, the brains, looks, personality, talents, parents, education, health, neighborhood, country, or times in which we live.

If inequality is synonymous with injustice, we live in a hopelessly unjust world. Are we going to try to level all these playing fields? And if so, how, and who will decide what is level? As economist Robert Sowell has observed:

> The difference between a factory worker and
> an executive is nothing compared to the dif-

ference between being born brain-damaged and being born normal, or the difference between being born to loving parents rather than abusive parents.[99]

If we are going to try to do something about this, we will first have to figure out how to measure the degree of brain damage or parental abuse. Then we will need to arrive at a reasonable compensation formula. Will we also try to provide equally good parents or equally good teachers for every child? Will we demand that Harvard University agree to teach any child who applies, and what will we do when we run out of Harvards assuming that we can still call it Harvard? Later in life, will we follow the now old people into their doctor's office to be sure that they all get exactly the same pill for the same malady, assuming that it is the same malady? If these examples seem far-fetched, it should be noted that contemporary philosophers have debated similar issues, because they do help us define what exactly we mean by equalitarianism.

Equalitarians might respond that, yes, the Jacobin idea of people being born equal is a fantasy, inequality is deeply imbedded in all life as we know it. But that is not a reason to abandon economic equality, it is all the more reason to pursue it. If life is inherently unequal, then let us make equal what we can, especially the economy, since that is the work of our own hands. But this too is easier said than done. If you give two individuals exactly the same income, one may save, invest, and grow rich, while the other may sink into torpor or debt. What is to be done then? Should we re-equalize the situation? How might that best be done?

There are additional complexities. To promote equality, one must be consistent, because inconsistent outcomes cannot be equal. But equalitarians are often inconsistent. They may prescribe heavy taxation on all incomes over X, which might be an average or a "middle-class" income of people in their own country. But, in doing so, they ignore the fact that a fifth of humanity is living on less than $1 a day,[100] that X may be a king's ransom in other, poorer countries. If redistributive policies are to be followed, why not apply them worldwide?

Similarly, some equalitarians may clamor for multinational companies to pay higher wages in poor countries, but then oppose free trade agreements that bring in more goods made by the same struggling wage-earners. In general, globalization and free trade should decrease inequality between countries, but may also reduce wages of the least skilled in rich countries, at least temporarily. Why do equalitarians notice the latter but not the former?

Consistency is one logical principle; clarity and completeness are others. To their critics, equalitarian arguments are unclear and incomplete, as well as inconsistent, because they fail to distinguish between unequal outcomes that change over time and unequal outcomes that are simply frozen. In traditional societies, inequality exists because of the lack of social mobility, that is, because positions are largely frozen. Free-market competition also creates economic inequality, but in the context of social mobility. Winners and losers change. Moreover, the social mobility implicit in free-market competition tends to reduce inequality over time, not increase it, as is commonly alleged. Economist Milton Friedman has observed that

> The development of [free markets] has greatly lessened the extent of inequality.... [101] Nowhere is the gap between rich and poor wider, nowhere are the rich richer and the poor poorer, than in those countries that do not permit the free market to operate. [102]

It should be readily apparent that economic equality, the equality of result, is incompatible with equality of opportunity. Most honest people will see advantages to both. But we must choose. We cannot have both, and if we have more of one we must accept less of the other.

Argument 5: Milton Friedman's assertion that the development of free markets has reduced inequality, and thus helped the poor, is equivalent to saying that inequality reduces inequality.

It is nonsensical. Even if inequality promotes economic growth in some circumstances, which is unlikely, very little of that economic growth reaches the poor.

As Jeffrey Gates, head of the Shared Capitalism Institute, has said, "Capitalism does not raise all boats; it raises all yachts."[103]

Argument 6: Response.

Economist Steve H. Hanke responds to Jeffrey Gates by citing a World Bank study by David Dollar and Aart Kraay. This study looked at eighty countries over four decades and concluded that free markets help "the poor" as much as the "non-poor." In addition, Dollar and Kraay found that the poor are especially benefited by controlling inflation and also by controlling the growth of government spending. Why government spending? As Hanke puts it, "The rich are much better placed to feed at the public trough. The poor get crumbs."[104]

We might also recall that, precisely because money means more to the poor than the rich, a rise in incomes through economic growth helps the poor disproportionately. The rich, earning more, buy luxuries they could already have bought if they had really wanted them. Or more likely they increase their saving, which helps everyone. The poor, earning more, can afford more necessities, or even some luxuries of their own. As Henry Hazlitt reminds us:

> The overwhelming majority of Americans . . . now enjoy the advantages of running

water, central heating, telephones, automobiles, refrigerators, washing machines, [music players], radios, television sets—amenities that millionaires and kings did not enjoy a few generations ago.[105]

Indeed, a study by the Heritage Foundation found that 41% of the official poor in the United States owned their own home. A majority owned automobiles as well as microwaves, DVD players, and air conditioning.

Argument 7: Response.

Even if all this were true, that equalitarian policies slow economic growth and ultimately retard the progress of the poor, would that invalidate the idea of sharing at least some of the wealth more equally now? Economist Arthur Okun, a former chairman of the President's Council of Economic Advisors, said that "I would prefer . . . complete [economic] equality."[106]

But he has also suggested that trading off some "growth" for some "equity" is a reasonable compromise, an idea seconded by another former CEA chair, economist Alan Blinder, who similarly speaks of reconciling "Principles of efficiency [with] principles of equity"[107] through tax and other policy adjustments.

Argument 8: Response.

Equalitarians like to think of the economy as a

machine with bells, whistles, and levers, all of which can be manipulated to produce more of this or less of that. But this is an illusion. As thinker and writer Irving Kristol has observed, "If you want economic growth, only that species of activity called 'business' can get it for you. The 'economy,' as conventionally understood, cannot."[108]

What this means is that, to have more economic growth, you must support businessmen or women, and demotivating them or reducing the savings available to them through income redistribution schemes will not help. Moreover, once you start down this path, intending to go only a short distance, it is often very hard to stop, for reasons explained by economist Sanford Ikeda: "Redistributional policies . . . typically aggravate the . . . problems . . . thereby providing even greater justification for more intervention."[109]

Argument 9: Response.

Income and wealth inequality is in fact increasing, especially in the United States, as confirmed by a succession of studies. The 1994 *Economic Report of the President*, written by the President's Council of Economic Advisors, drew upon some of these studies to state unequivocally that "Starting some time in the late 1970s, income inequalities widened alarmingly in America."[110]

Is society, acting through government, to stand back and do nothing about this?

Argument 10: Response.

What is probably happening is that the emergence of a truly global economy is reducing global inequality by increasing incomes in developing countries. Unfortunately, as part of this, some lower-paid workers in developed countries are struggling. But even this is only a guess. Most of the studies purportedly showing an increase of income inequality in the United States are based on questionable data.

For example, government personal income data is distorted because many businesses report on personal rather than corporate income tax forms and this trend is sharply increasing, primarily because of the growing use of Limited Liability Companies (LLCs) as the favored form of business organization. When income that used to be reported on corporate returns as corporate income is shifted to personal returns, it can seem that high-end incomes are growing more rapidly than they really are.

Government income data is collected by household, but household size changes a great deal over time, which makes it difficult to see what is happening to individuals. Age is also very important: the same individual may be counted as poor as a student, rich in middle age, and poor again in old age, so changes in the average age of the population skew results. Immigration is rarely considered in income inequality statistics. But immigrants, especially in the U.S., tend to start out as very poor and this can distort what is happening in the bottom decile or quintile.

The way income is defined matters a great deal. Government statistics vary considerably in what they include or exclude, and the decisions often make no sense. For example, transfer payments such as the earned income tax credit, welfare payments, and social security income are not counted. One of the worst mistakes is treating a capital gain as personal income. When people sell a stock, receive cash, and realize a capital gain (that is, sell an asset for more than it cost), they actually exchange one asset for another rather than create economic income (see Appendix B). It would also help to know how many hours people work for their income. If person A works 40 hours and person B works 80 hours, most people would not think it unequal for B to be paid twice as much.

In any case, none of the available U.S. government statistics exclude business income and provide reliable per capita (per person), age-adjusted, immigration-adjusted, work-hour-adjusted, income-definition-adjusted data. Without this information, it is reasonable to think that income inequality has been increasing in the United States, but it cannot be proven one way or the other.

Part Eight

Greed

16

Does the Profit System Glorify Greed?—Yes

EQUALITARIANS HAVE NO DOUBTS: free markets not only teach, they demand greed. Opponents of equalitarianism, by contrast, speak with conflicting voices. Some say, yes, a private market system is grounded in greed, and that is a good thing. A larger number reject the word greed, but see nothing wrong with acting in your own self-interest. A minority argue that the whole question is muddled, that a private market system is grounded neither in greed nor in self-interest, but rather teaches people to think of others, to practice social virtues, not vices. We will listen briefly to each of these arguments.

Argument 1: Private markets are indeed grounded in selfishness and greed and are thus inherently immoral.

Private markets not only tolerate naked greed, sharp practice, acquisitiveness, predation, exploitation, commercialism, and materialism. They positively encourage all these evils. In the words of the *Communist Manifesto*, they plunge us into "the icy water of egotistical calculation."[111]

Anacharsis of Scythia warned as early as the seventh century B.C.E. that "The market is a place set apart where men may deceive one another,"[112] a sentiment seconded by Aristotle and many others. In 1933, at the bottom of the Great Depression, Matthew Josephson suggested in his book, *The Robber Barons*, that slavery was not the only contradiction marring the otherwise remarkable story of American economic development:

> To organize and exploit the resources of a nation upon a gigantic scale, to regiment its farmers and workers into harmonious corps of producers, and to do this only in the name of an uncontrolled appetite for private profit—here surely is the great inherent contradiction whence so much disaster, outrage and misery has flowed.[113]

The misery still flows, and it is time, as playwright Tony Kushner told a graduating class of college seniors, to stand up for

> The people and not the oil plutocrats, ... the
> multivarious multicultural people and not the
> pale, pale, cranky, grim, greedy people, ... the
> hard-working people and not the people
> whose only real exertion ever in their parasite
> lives has been the effort it takes to [get poli-
> ticians to] slash a trillion dollars in tax reve-
> nue and then stuff it in their already overfull
> pockets.[114]

The problem is not just that some people, given a chance to be greedy, will grind others into the dirt. The problem is the market system itself. Hence, as Bill Moyers, one-time presidential assistant and promi-nent public television voice, has argued, we must guard against "true believers in the God of the market who would leave us to the ruthless forces of unfettered monopolistic capital where even the laws of the jungle break down."[115]

Moreover, as Moyers continues, these market idola-tors may wrap themselves in the (American) flag and rely "on your patriotism to distract you from their plunder. While you're standing at attention with your hand over your heart pledging allegiance to the flag, they're picking your pocket."[116]

This is all the more ironic because, as Lawrence Kaplan, has argued:

> The market erodes national sovereignty ... ,
> and, with it, much of the State's legitimate

authority. [If this process is not arrested], market identity [may] supersede civic virtue and national allegiance [as well as] foster . . . widespread atomism.[117]

Markets are inescapably immoral, and if we cannot eliminate them, we should at least not glorify them. Marcia Angell, former editor-in-chief of the prestigious *New England Journal of Medicine*, recalls that before the 1980s:

There was something faintly disreputable about really big fortunes. You could choose to do well or you could choose to do good. . . . That belief was particularly strong among scientists and other intellectuals.[118]

It is important to stand up to what President Franklin Roosevelt referred to as "money changers in the temple" and "malefactors of great wealth" But it is also important to recognize, and guard against, the greed that lies within each of us. No one living in an economically developed country can completely escape the charge of greed, because no one can completely avoid participating in a market system that thrives on waste, that ignores the sustainability of resources, notwithstanding the fragility of our increasingly crowded and overtaxed planet. As Bernard Muller has said, in a letter to the editor of *World Watch* magazine:

Against . . . growth-mania, we have as yet only a disarray of sustainability supporters. Not one government, not one country has renounced growth. . . . Society and governments must urgently intervene to impose upon the market . . . the objective of negative growth in physical resource use.[119]

17

Does the Profit System Glorify Greed?—Yes, and a Good Thing

Argument 2: "Greed is good."

SELFISHNESS IS A given, is it not? Why be holier-than-thou? Does not Jennifer Beth Cohen speak for all of us when she states in her book, *My Russian Affair*, that

> Everyone's life is all about himself or herself. That doesn't mean that your concerns are all selfish or that you can't or don't care about others. But in the end it does come back to you, doesn't it?[120]

One can alternatively argue that greed and aggression are not perhaps desirable in themselves, but still necessary for economic progress, a position that many commentators have taken:

■■ "The greatest meliorator of the world is selfish, huckstering trade." (Ralph Waldo Emerson, *Work and Days*)[121]

■■ "[I]t is precisely the 'greed' of the businessman or, more appropriately, his profit-seeking, which is the unexcelled protection of the consumer." (Alan Greenspan, "The Assault on Integrity")[122]

Economist John Maynard Keynes, by no means in the "greed is good" camp, thought that greed was useful, at least for now:

> Avarice and usury must be our gods for a little longer still. For only they can lead us out of the tunnel of economic necessity into daylight.[123]

The most forceful exponent of the "greed-is-good" philosophy, novelist Ayn Rand, held that greed is only menacing outside market environments:

> When money ceases to be the tool by which men deal with one another, then men become the tools of men. Blood, whips, guns—or dollars. Take your choice.[124]

Channeled appropriately through markets, even the

most immoderate greed (according to Rand) is only beneficent:

> America's abundance was not created by public sacrifices to "the common good," but by the productive genius of free men who pursued their own personal interests and the making of their own private fortunes. They did not starve the people to pay for America's industrialization. They gave the people better jobs, higher wages, and cheaper goods.[125]

Indeed, Rand insisted, the selfishness of the rich and powerful is not even very selfish, properly understood:

> The man at the top of the intellectual pyramid contributes the most to all those below him, but gets nothing except his material payment, receiving no intellectual bonus from others. . . . The man at the bottom who, left to himself, would starve . . . , contributes nothing [intellectually] to those above him, but receives the bonus of all their brains.[126]

Before leaving this particular segment of our debate, we should note in passing that there are numerous philosophical disputes flickering in the background, technical philosophical disputes among rational choice theorists, welfare economists, and many others about whether it is possible to define concepts such as greed, selfishness, altruism, the collective good, and if so, how to go about it.

18

Does the Profit System Glorify Greed?—No

Argument 3: Whether one disapproves or approves of greed, it is quite erroneous to think that markets encourage it. Markets are just technical, and thus morally neutral, mechanisms for human exchange.

SOCIAL PHILOSOPHER DANIEL Bell described markets as a "techno-economic structure."[127]

Milton Friedman took the same position when he said that "[What is often referred to as the market] ethic . . . cannot in and of itself be regarded as an ethical principle; it must be regarded as . . . a corollary of some other principle such as freedom."[128]

Argument 4: No, the market is not morally neutral, it does express an ethical principle, and that principle is certainly not greed. It is instead rational self-interest, something quite different from greed, and this is by far the best principle on which to organize a society.

A defense of rational self-interest was memorably offered by the economist Adam Smith in the eighteenth century:

> It is not from the benevolence of the butcher, the brewer, or the baker, that we expect our dinner, but from their regard to their own interest. We address ourselves, not to their humanity but to their self-love, and never talk to them of our own necessities but of their advantages.[129]

> ... He generally, indeed, neither intends to promote the public interest, nor knows how much he is promoting it. ... He intends only his own gain, and he is in this, as in many other cases, led by an invisible hand to promote an end which was no part of his intention.[130]

The all-important distinction in Smith's system is between rational and irrational self-interest. The world has had many economic systems based on irrational self-interest, and these bring only misery. For example, consider economic historian David Landes's description of the Ottoman (Turkish) empire of the fourteenth–early twentieth centuries:

The Ottomans had . . . taken over a region once strong, now enfeebled—looting as they went. Now they could no longer take from outside. They had to generate wealth from within, to promote productive investment. Instead, they resorted to habit and tried to pillage the interior, to squeeze their own subjects. Nothing, not even the wealth of high officials, was secure. Nothing could be more self-destructive.[131]

In Adam Smith's and his successors' view, it was the development of free markets that made rational (as distinct from irrational) self-interest possible. Walter Lippmann explained this idea:

Until the division of labor had begun to make men dependent upon the free collaboration of other men, the worldly policy was to be predatory. The claims of the spirit were other-worldly. So it was not until the industrial revolution had altered the traditional mode of life that the vista was opened at the end of which men could see the possibility of the Good Society on this earth. At long last the ancient schism between the world and the spirit, between self-interest and disinterestedness, was potentially closed, and a wholly new orientation of the human race became theoretically conceivable and, in fact, necessary.[132]

The stress on rational self-interest also helps to explain why free markets are supposed to be "dog eat dog," but are often quite civil and peaceful, indeed more civil and peaceful than authoritarian alternatives. Adam Smith (and many others) stressed that rational self-interest is often a powerful tutor of personal and civic virtues:

> Whenever commerce is introduced into any country, probity[,] . . . punctuality[,] . . . economy, industry, [and] discretion . . . always accompany it. These virtues in a rude and barbarous country are almost unknown.[133, 134]

Economist David Levy takes this further. Hope for personal gain may powerfully motivate us to pay attention to the needs and wishes of others:

> Under [the profit system], even an insensitive man who would not pause to help a blind person across the street develops an interest in other people's wants and whims when he contemplates investing in a business.[135]

Argument 5: The private market system is grounded neither in greed nor in self-interest.

Adam Smith seriously erred in suggesting that it was, and his authority has misled us for centuries. The market system teaches naturally selfish people to put aside their selfishness and practice some of the "highest" values of social cooperation that human beings have ever achieved.

"Market values" are the diametrical opposite of "every man for himself." The "self-interest model" so beloved of economists is completely illusory. A young person may proclaim: I will start my own business in order to be my own boss. But if he or she persists in this illusion, the new business will fail, as most do. In order to start and run a successful business, one must be willing, above all, to subordinate oneself in the service of others. One must serve one's customers and one must also serve and respect and nurture one's employees.

Sometimes "bosses" are so talented or lucky that they do well without fully learning these lessons. Even then, they do not do nearly as well as they might have. The iron rule is: everything else being equal, the better you serve, the better you do. Predation, exploitation, parasitism, or greed may make this transaction, or even this year's profits, fatter. But a business is defined as the present value of all future profits, and these true profits are ruined by selfishness, even so-called "rational" selfishness.

"Market" values are not easy. They are extremely demanding, and in many cases take generations to learn. Nor are they "lower than" or "separate from" religious values. It is true that they are not identical to religious values, but they are rather "complementary" to religion and have arguably done as much as religion to "civilize" us, especially given the dark side of religion exemplified by religious wars. It is no coincidence that it was defenders of free markets who led the battle against world slavery and finally won it, against large odds, in the nineteenth century. As economist George Stigler writes:

> Important as the moral influences of the market place are, they have not been subjected to any real study. The immense proliferation of general education, of scientific progress, and of democracy are all coincidental in time and place with the emergence of the free enterprise system of organizing the market place. I believe this coincidence was not accidental.[136]

A critic of free markets, Liah Greenfield, has asserted in her book, *The Spirit of Capitalism: Nationalism and Economic Growth*, that nationalism promotes free-market growth. The truth is just the opposite: "market values" are at odds with nationalism, tribalism, racism, and sectarianism of all kinds, and continually teach us to tolerate, work with, and ultimately appreciate people wherever and however we find them.

The hostile attitude of most economists toward the idea of the market as a source of moral values is hard to fathom, although it may simply reflect a lack of personal familiarity with business. Listen to Geoffrey Martin Hodgson:

> The firm has to compete not simply for profit but for our confidence and trust. To achieve

this, it has to abandon profit-maximisation, or even shareholder satisfaction, as the exclusive objectives of the organization.[137]

This is quite wrong. In truth, confidence and trust do not in the least conflict with profits. On the contrary, one cannot have the latter without the former, as great businesses have shown throughout history.

Perhaps the ultimate wrong note of this kind was sounded by economist John Kenneth Galbraith, past president of the American Economics Association, when he wrote that:

> There is nothing reliable to be learned about making money. If there were, study would be intense and everyone with a positive IQ would be rich.[138]

What Galbraith, like others, failed to see is that one does not necessarily need a high IQ to make money, but rather the right personal values, in particular an ardor to serve others and a degree of realism about how to do it (since in markets, as in life generally, good intentions alone do not suffice).

Many economists do, of course, see morality in markets, if not perhaps the very highest morality. For example, *The Economist* comments on a study by Cornell economists Robert Frank, Thomas Gilovich, and Dennis Regan:

> Imagine a world in which people move from one prisoner's dilemma to the next (i.e., the

real world). If people can choose their "partners" freely, and if honest types can spot each
other in advance, co-operators will be able
to interact selectively with each other—and
will therefore do better than cheats. Experi-
ments have shown that people are surprisingly good at telling co-operators and cheats
apart, even on the basis of what seems to be
limited information.

So there you have it: narrowly self-interested
behaviour is ultimately self-defeating.[139]

Part Nine

Government

19

Can Government Protect Us from the Excesses of the Profit System?—Yes

T HE QUESTION POSED ABOVE has been formally debated for at least two thousand years. We know this because ancient Chinese annals record the then controversial decision of the powerful Han emperor Wu-di (155–87 B.C.E.) to take a more direct hand in guiding and regulating the economy, and in particular to establish government monopolies of certain key commodities such as salt, iron, and alcohol.

Professor Kenneth J. Hammond of New Mexico State University, speaking in a college course lecture, describes these new government monopolies in approving terms:

> Wu-di wants the government ... to solve problems for people.... What Wu-di was against was the manipulation of the market by private interests to enrich themselves, in other words, he was against mercantile profiteering.... [Consequently] production ... [and] distribution [of salt, iron, alcohol] was controlled by the state, so that ... these things that were needed by everybody could be afforded by everybody.... The state [thus] becomes an agency for fostering and creating the good life [with] the job of ... regulat[ing] private greed and insur[ing] that ... ordinary people are protected and ... are not subject to the exploitation of greedy merchants.[140]

In ancient China, it was highly imprudent to criticize the emperor openly, but one of Wu-di's advisors, Sima Qian, did just that. He wrote:

> What need is there for government [economic] directives [or monopolies]? Each man has only to be left to utilize his own abilities and exert his strength to obtain what he wishes. Thus, when a commodity is very cheap, it invites a rise in price; when it is very expensive, it invites a reduction. When each person works away at his own occupation and delights in his own business then, like water flowing downward, goods will naturally flow forth ceaselessly day and night without hav-

ing been summoned, and the people will produce commodities without having been asked. Does this not tally with reason? Is it not a natural result?[141]

Wu-di was not pleased with this response, and castrated Sima for daring to speak his mind. But the debate did not die, either in ancient China or in other countries and eras.

Sir Francis Brewster, a seventeenth-century English writer, was quite unaware of the Han dynasty controversy, but nevertheless offered a rebuttal of Sima's position in 1702: "Trade indeed will find its own Channels, but it may be the ruin of the Nation, if not Regulated."[142]

Later in the same century, the economist Adam Smith rebutted Brewster and restated Sima's case in words strikingly reminiscent of the early Chinese master's own:

> The natural effort of every individual to better his own condition, when suffered to exert itself with freedom and security, is . . . not only capable of carrying on the society to wealth and prosperity, but of surmounting an hundred impertinent obstructions with which the folly of human laws too often encumbers its operations.[143]

We have already touched on this fundamental debate about government regulation and leadership of the economy in some prior chapters, especially in Part Five. Now, in Parts Nine and Ten, we will discuss it directly from a variety of angles.

Argument 1: A private profit-making economy without government regulation is unbearable.

Recall for a moment the kind of unregulated labor conditions described by historian David Landes in turn-of-the-twentieth-century Argentina:

> In the textile, metal, match, and glass factories, the air was always full of a fine dust that irritated the lungs. In leather factories, the curing process required the use of sulfuric, nitric, and muriatic acids as well as arsenic and ammonia, all of which gave off harmful vapors that filled the building. In the packinghouses, workers trod upon floors that were slippery with coagulated blood, entrails, and animal excrement. The stench was overwhelming. The men who carried meat to the freezers had to wrap their hands and faces in rags or old newspapers...lest...fresh blood...freeze to their bodies.[144]

In unregulated, "sink or swim" markets, women and children suffer even more than men. In early-twentieth-century New York, 146 female workers, mostly immigrant, all desperately poor, perished in the Triangle Shirtwaist Factory fire because their employer had locked the doors to prevent unauthorized work breaks or theft. Civilized communities should never accept such conditions—the full force of law must be brought to bear to prevent them. But similar travesties continue to this day.

Toward the close of the twentieth century, pygmies in central Africa were working all day for logging companies in exchange for two cigarettes. These were what defenders of completely free markets call "voluntary transactions," which they assume by definition to make both parties better off. But no reasonable person can argue that the pygmies were better off for these transactions, no matter how voluntary, any more than the nineteenth century Chinese paid by British merchants in opium were better off for theirs.

Argument 2: Protecting workers is only the beginning of what the community, acting through government, must do.

From the late nineteenth century on, progressives and other critics of private profit-making markets have gradually developed a broad program calling for the state to:

- ▦ Protect the powerless, disabled, minorities, children, and women, and reduce economic inequality;
- ▦ Provide public education and health services, standards, and mandates;

∷ Regulate and control greed and selfishness among private interests, especially corporations and the rich, and ensure that businesses provide safe working conditions, produce safe consumer products, and stop polluting the environment;

∷ Take full responsibility for national employment levels and control of the business cycle.

By the end of the twentieth century, virtually all political parties in the world, and especially those intent on winning democratic elections, took this program for granted, and so did government officials and central bankers. Even the parties that most publicly identified with free markets, such as the Republican Party in the U.S., firmly embraced it.

20

Can Government Protect Us from the Excesses of the Profit System?—No

Argument 3. Supporters of government intervention in the economy like to describe government as synonymous with community, a community of all citizens.

THIS IS FALSE. Government is not synonymous with community. Like other institutions, it looks upon the world through the lens of self-interest. And because it enjoys a monopoly of coercive force, it has the potential to be the worst predator of all.

We should not assume that government is less selfish, more altruistic, more driven by ideals of the common good than private markets, and is therefore the fittest agent of our community aspirations. All human institutions are flawed, because human beings are flawed, but government is more flawed and more dangerous than private markets.

We can walk away forever from a bad boss, merchant, or customer, but we cannot walk away from the government. Therein lies a paradox. We have concentrated power in public guardians in order to protect us from private violence, theft, and fraud. But, having done so, who will guard us from the guardians?

This is not a hypothetical problem. We began this book by asking why human beings have still not pulled themselves out of often desperate poverty after all these thousands of years of so-called civilized life. Until the eighteenth century, the human economy as a whole barely grew at all, and even since then the rate of growth has not been exceptional. Why is this? Economist John Maynard Keynes said that

> The destruction of the inducement to invest by [a tendency to keep what wealth one had under a mattress] was the outstanding evil, the prime impediment to the growth of wealth, in the ancient and medieval worlds.[145]

But what Keynes overlooked was that people hid their money because they feared theft, and they especially feared theft by government.

In Sung China (tenth century), merchants were classed with undertakers and other "unclean" groups,[146] and the government did not hesitate to confiscate mercantile fortunes that came to its attention, a pattern that persisted throughout Chinese imperial history. The great historian of commerce and capitalism, Fernand Braudel, acknowledges that

> In the vast world of Islam, especially prior to the eighteenth century, . . . ownership was temporary, for there, as in China, [property] . . . legally belonged to the prince. . . . When the [rich person] . . . died, his seigneury and all his possessions reverted to the Sultan of Istanbul or the Great Mogul of Delhi. . . . [147] [In addition,] André Raymond's recent study of eighteenth-century Cairo shows us that the great merchants there rarely were able to maintain their positions for more than a generation. They were devoured by political society.[148]

The historian David Landes records the same thing in Japan. He cites the case of Yodoya Tatsugoro, scion of the leading commercial family in Osaka. The family had made itself immensely rich, had also performed many services to the nation, and had regularly lent money to the ruling classes. These loans could not be refused, but once made, they led to strained relations. In the end, all the family's money was confiscated by the government on the grounds that Yodoya was "living beyond his social status."[149]

Since the eighteenth century, the record of capital accumulation has improved. Governments have gradually learned that it is better to pluck the goose than to kill it, and Lord Macaulay correctly observed that, at least in Britain:

> Profuse government expenditure, heavy taxation, absurd commercial restriction, corrupt tribunals, disastrous wars, . . . persecutions, conflagrations, inundations, have not been able to destroy capital so fast as the exertions of private citizens have been able to create it.[150]

Even so, humanity's capital continues to be very much at risk. If only the recurrent destructions of capital by government can be avoided, the world might yet be awash with wealth. Every child might be, in financial writer James Grant's words, "a trust-fund baby."[151]

Argument 4: Government is also corrupt.

The primary charge against government is that it is predatory, a devourer of society's capital. But predation is not the whole story. More often than not, government is also corrupt. Moreover, the opportunities for corruption multiply the more deeply government gets into the economy.

To be sure, the line between predation and corruption may be indistinct. Demanding a bribe is both predatory and corrupt. Supporting private-market predators, such as trial lawyers, in return for financial support is also predatory and corrupt. But the heart of government corruption lies in the "soft" bribery of ordinary interest-group politics.

This is familiar ground, but some of the deals worked out between politicians and special interests may be complex and only later reveal their true nature. For example, large U.S. tobacco companies were supposedly punished for deceiving the public about smoking risks when they agreed in 1998 to pay 46 states and their lawyers hundreds of billions of dollars in fines over 25 years. In fact a tacit deal was struck in which the same states agreed to limit new entrants into the tobacco business. The existing companies then used their newly protected cartel status to raise prices repeatedly, in unison, thereby generating far more money than was needed for the fines, money that flowed directly into profits.

Not surprisingly, Milton Friedman argues that "Probably the most important source of monopoly power has been government assistance, direct and indirect."[152]

Businesses are among the most important special interests, but so are unions and trial lawyers, each of which also benefit from government monopoly grants and licensing restrictions.

Politicians and their clients are the central figures in interest-group politics, but there are other, almost equally important figures, such as regulators, heads of interest group organizations, and lobbyists. For example, the U.S. Department of Agriculture is supposed to protect the public from contaminated meat. But when small meat producers proposed to test each cow slaughtered for mad cow disease, a deadly illness transferable to humans, the Department repeatedly ruled in the early 2000s that such testing, if done, could not be communicated to customers. In issuing this edict, the department sided with large meat producers who not only wished to avoid the cost of testing, but also wanted to use the power of government to prevent smaller producers from gaining an advantage from it. The regulators clearly saw large meat packers, not the general public, as their clients.[153]

Sometimes "little deals" between regulators and powerful commercial interests have very large historical consequences. For example, in seventeenth- and eighteenth-century France, the rich woolen, silk, and linen producers persuaded the government to ban the production of cotton cloth, which was then a new product. On one level, this produced rather comical results as government spies began "peering into coaches and private houses and reporting that the governess of the Marquis de Cormoy had been seen at her window clothed in calico of a white background with big red flowers, almost new."[154]

All was not gossip and amusement, however. Enforcement of the rules led many thousands of ordinary people to be executed or sent into gruesome labor on ships. Perhaps most importantly, Britain created its industrial revolution and surged ahead economically by producing cotton textiles, while France's refusal to allow cotton meant that it stagnated and fell far behind.

Argument 5: A government that is neither predatory nor corrupt can be of immense help to an economy.

The case for a state that acts only as an economic umpire, not an economic leader, that scrupulously limits itself to setting rules that apply to everyone, that does not try to intervene to assist any person or persons, or otherwise pursue its own aims and objectives—that case has been made in France and in many other countries. Boisguilbert asked the French government in the early eighteenth century to "*laissez-faire la nature*," by which he meant to get out of the way of commerce.[155]

Jeremy Bentham asked the British and other governments to "be quiet."[156] Economist Ludwig von Mises denied that a limited government is that "which governs least," because the state should strenuously "protect the smooth functioning of the market economy against fraud or violence from within or from without the country,"[157] an idea echoed by Harvard philosopher Robert Nozick.

Advocates of laissez-faire have become accustomed to having their words fall on deaf ears. Not long before

the French Revolution, Jacques Turgot was appointed
Comptroller-General of France and tried in twenty
brief months to reform the tottering economic system along free-market lines. But he was forced to
resign, thereby sealing the fate of Louis XVI and the
old regime. In 1770, Turgot said wryly of his friend de
Gournay:

> He was … astonished to see the [French
> monarchy] … fancy … that it ensured abun-
> dance of grain by making the condition of the
> cultivator more uncertain and unhappy than
> that of all other citizens.[158]

A few years later, Étienne Bonnot, the Abbé de Condillac, exclaimed that "experience teaches [govern-
ment] nothing. How many mistakes have been made!
How many times have they been repeated! And they
are still repeated!"[159]

One can only imagine what the Abbé de Condillac would have thought of life at the beginning of the
twenty-first century in Zimbabwe, a country once
described as the "breadbasket" of Africa, but which
writhed in misery under the iron grip of Robert
Mugabe's government. Land redistribution schemes
had turned over much of the best cropland to Mugabe
supporters who had not the slightest knowledge of
farming. As a result, over half of the country's 12 mil-
lion people were on the brink of starvation. In many
cases, government opponents were forcibly relocated

to remote rural areas with no means of subsistence at all.

In towns, gasoline supplies had long since disappeared, although rumors caused people periodically to race to closed pumps to see if anything had arrived. Everything was price controlled, often at a price well below the cost of production. To avoid evasion of the price controls, no "new" product, brand, or packaging could be sold without prior written permission from one of the ministries. The economy as a whole was estimated to be imploding at a rate of 10% a year, but property and market values had already lost 99% of their previous value.[160] Throughout all this, Mugabe gave speeches railing against "greedy entrepreneurs, ruthless markets and the forces of globalization."[161]

At the end of the twentieth century, some free-market economists tried to offer broad-based statistical studies purporting to show that government leadership of the economy was a losing proposition. One study looked at 115 countries, ranked each country by measures of government intervention, and concluded that per capita gross domestic product was negatively correlated with such intervention.[162] Another study found a similar negative correlation between government spending as a percent of GDP and GDP growth.[163] Yet a third study found that the poor especially benefited from less government intrusion.[164]

The problem with all such studies is of course that they can and will be rebutted by someone else's study.

The misleading idea, as economist Israel Kirzner puts it, that, "Chaos and misery [are] ... bound to ensue unless market forces are curbed, redirected or superseded by the firm, benevolent hand of an all-wise government,"[165] is simply too entrenched in the human psyche to be displaced by statistical evidence.

A few committed believers in government leadership of the economy are willing to admit that their ideas have not lived up to expectations. The leading British socialist Aneurin Bevin quipped at a Labour Party Conference in 1945 that "only an organizing genius could produce a shortage of coal and fish in Britain."[166]

Walter Lippmann, a progressive who was always sympathetic to the idea of government economic leadership, and kept looking for ways to make it work, admitted that it tended to produce the opposite of what was expected:

> This is the vicious paradox of the gradual collectivism which has developed in western society during the past sixty years: it has provoked the expectation of universal plenty provided by action of the state while, through almost every action undertaken or tolerated by the state, the production of wealth is restricted.[167]

Nevertheless, as von Mises pointed out:

> Government interference with business is

still very popular. As soon as someone does not like something that happens in the world, he says: "The government ought to do something about it. What do we have a government for?"[168]

Philosopher Michael Novak, who once believed in state leadership himself, shakes his head at this:

> One of the most astonishing characteristics of our age is that ideas, even false and unworkable ideas, even ideas which are no longer believed in by their official guardians, rule the affairs of men and run roughshod over stubborn facts. Ideas of enormous destructiveness, cruelty, and impracticality retain the allegiance of elites that benefit from them[169] . . . . [or feel that abandoning them would] violate . . . a taboo.[170]

Novak emphasizes that, in his view, it is the poorest who suffer from our mental sclerosis:

> [The] suffering [of poverty] is unnecessary because over the centuries a [free-market] system has been worked out to create "the wealth of nations"—all nations. To bring that system to all the world's poor is . . . our chief unfinished business.[171]

Argument 6: Response.

And what would Novak say to Hillary Clinton, senator from New York, who warned in her memoirs that:

> I do believe there was, and still is, an interlocking network of groups and individuals who want to turn the clock back on many of the advances our country has made, from civil rights and women's rights to consumer and environmental regulation, and they use all the tools at their disposal—money, power, influence, media and politics—to achieve their ends.[172]

Part Ten

Central Banks

21

Can Central Banks Protect Us from the Excesses of the Profit System and Lead the Economy?—Yes

ALTHOUGH GOVERNMENTS ARE in charge of a nation's money, they usually delegate day-to-day control to a central bank. The central bank will then decide whether there is too much or too little money in circulation, whether money market (short-term) interest rates are at an appropriate level, whether the banking system is operating safely and smoothly, and so on. In most cases, the central bank will also directly supervise and regulate private banks.

As a general rule, political progressives are supporters of central banks, because they favor more government leadership of the economy, assume that economic conditions will lapse into chaos without such leadership, and think that central bankers are more qualified to carry out this critical task than politicians. Laissez-faire advocates, by contrast, take a dim view of this, since they think that the government should not try to lead the economy. Nor are they convinced that central bankers will be that much wiser or successful than politicians.

Argument 1: Without a central bank, there would be no way to control the dangerous excesses of the banking system and otherwise keep the economy on a steady course.

The U.S. Panic of 1907 provided some of the impetus for the Federal Reserve Act of 1913. Although the 1907 panic was unusually severe, it was only the latest in a long series of such episodes. As the *Washington Post* pointed out in an editorial:

> The world's . . . history . . . [has been] a succession of panics, slumps, and crashes in which markets were working, all right—but working as they sometimes do, perversely and blindly.[173]

The creators of the Federal Reserve hoped that it would prevent both bank excesses and bank runs, and by doing so help stabilize the economy. Despite uncertainties about how "loose" or "tight" monetary policy should be, the U.S. "Fed," as it is commonly called, has been a signal success. Economic writer Jeff Madrick states that "By 1913 the U.S. federal government created a stable financial system with the creation of the Federal Reserve."[174]

Given the convulsions of the Great Depression, economist Geoffrey Moore, architect of the government's index of leading economic indicators, offers a sensible qualification: "I think in general the Federal Reserve has had a stabilizing effect on the economy, especially since World War II."[175]

George Moore, who built the banking colossus Citibank, agreed and added that "The Federal Reserve has learned that at the very least you have to put a floor under the economy [by expanding the money supply whenever deflation threatens]."[176]

Alan Greenspan's long eighteen-year tenure as Federal Reserve Chairman at the end of the twentieth century and the start of the twenty-first has been particularly singled out for praise. Employment during that period remained high, inflation averaged less than 3% a year, and the chairman earned, in economist Robert Solow's words, "Massive respect, even awe. . . ."[177]

Some observers did express concern about the growing

U.S. trade and current account deficits* of the Greenspan era. Because the U.S. was buying far more from foreigners than it was selling, it was borrowing more and more to pay for the purchases. In many cases, the same foreigners who sold the goods provided the financing.†

Worry about mounting U.S. international debts was natural, but it was wrong. Trade and current account deficits do not really matter; it is probably a waste of effort even to measure them. The U.S. ran in the red in both accounts for its first century. By the 1890s, for-eigners owned sizeable minority and even majority stakes in the largest American companies, especially the railroads.[178] What harm did this do? Only thirty years later, circumstances had reversed and Europe-ans were borrowing from America. We should not pay much attention to global financial flows and who owns what at any given moment.

---

* A trade deficit occurs when a country buys more goods from abroad than it sells. A current account deficit occurs when more money flows out than flows in and reflects a wide variety of transactions including products, services, foreign investment income, corporate profits earned abroad (and repatriated), and so on.

† International seller financing works as follows. Assume that a Chinese company sells some goods to the U.S. The American party pays in dol-lars, the Chinese company takes the dollars to the Chinese central bank and is given Chinese remnimbi, currency that has either been borrowed from domestic savers or that has been newly created for this purpose. The Chinese central bank then commonly invests the dollars by buy-ing U.S. bonds through the U.S. Federal Reserve. To the degree that new remnimbi have been created, they increase the Chinese domes-tic money supply, and all else being equal, increase the likelihood of domestic Chinese inflation.

It is also important to emphasize that the U.S., as a global currency reserve country,[‡] is able to borrow in its own currency, in dollars. This is unusual—most countries have to borrow money denominated in a foreign currency. Then, if the value of their own money falls in relation to the foreign currency, the amount of money owed can explode. By contrast, the U.S. need not worry, since it can repay its debt in dollars, can even print new dollars for this purpose. If foreigners who have lent money to the U.S. lose confidence in the dollar, the international value of the dollar will fall. But that hurts the foreign lenders, not the American borrowers. All the U.S. has to do is to ignore financial writer James K. Glassman's odd advice to borrow in yen, since the U.S. cannot print its own yen, and all should be well.[179]

U.S. economist Merton Miller has explained the situation clearly:

> We've actually been playing a cruel trick on the Japanese [and Chinese]. We've persuaded them to send us expensive [goods]—and in exchange we give them pictures of George Washington. . . . [If] they want . . . their money . . . , "Okay," we say, . . . "[but if you try to sell the U.S. currency that we give you on

---

[‡] A global currency reserve country issues currency that other central banks are willing to hold in their financial reserves, and which both governments and businesses all over the world use in their financial transactions.

world markets, you may only get] 20 cents on the dollar." They're the losers at this game.[180]

Economist Paul McCulley agreed:

To those with Calvinistic tendencies, always looking for what can go wrong, . . . the notion of . . . [the United States financing its consumption by borrowing from China] just doesn't seem right. . . . But . . . [at least for the moment] it is good, very good.[181]

22

Can Central Banks Protect Us from the Excesses of the Profit System and Lead the Economy?—No

Argument 2: The record of the U.S. Federal Reserve has been poor. The country did much better before its founding.

FROM THE END of the U.S. Civil War to the founding of the Federal Reserve almost a half century later in 1913–14, consumer prices fell more years than they rose, but ended up about where they started. This was a time of excellent economic and employment growth and also included some of the best stock market returns. At least one study of stock returns from 1872 showed that periods of mild deflation, such as we had in the latter half of the nineteenth century, have produced the best stock market returns of all, even better than periods of mild inflation.[182]

Shortly after the founding of the Fed, inflation surged. This was generally explained by the need to finance World War One. After that war ended, prices fell again, although not to pre-war levels. They declined gently during the 1920s, fell dramatically during the Great Depression (but again not to pre–World War One levels), rose during World War Two despite price controls, continued to rise after the war, and then surged again in the 1960s and 1970s. At the very end of the 1970s, the Fed under chairman Paul Volcker seemed to declare war on inflation, and double digit inflation rates fell dramatically. But in the quarter century following, consumer prices doubled again. All in all, during the first ninety years of the Fed, the U.S. dollar lost 95% of its purchasing power.

Federal legislation requires the Fed to control inflation. Successive chairmen and board members have repeatedly affirmed this objective, and there is no doubt that the Fed could stop inflation if it wished to. All it would have to do is print less new money. As production grew without new money being created, the ratio of goods to money would increase which would mean more goods for less money or, in other words, lower prices.

Yet by the early twenty-first century, the board was pursuing an unacknowledged two percent inflation target similar to the European Central Bank's acknowledged 2% target. Since the price of manufactured goods was generally falling, an overall rise in prices could only be engineered by subsidizing the relative lack of productivity and oversize price increases in services such as healthcare, housing, and education.

In 1985, Thibaut de Saint Phalle, author of *The Federal Reserve: An Intentional Mystery*, wrote that:

> It is puzzling that no one in Congress ever points out that it is the Fed itself that creates inflation and, more recently, permits Congress to ignore the growing budget deficits. The Fed, by financing the federal deficit year after year, makes it possible for Congress to continue to spend far more than it collects in tax revenues. If it were not for Fed action, Congress would have to curb its spending habits dramatically.[183]

Economist Murray Rothbard thought that there was no mystery about the Fed at all:

> If the chronic inflation undergone by Americans, and in almost every other country, is caused by the continuing creation of new

money, and if in each country its governmental "central bank" (in the United States, the Federal Reserve) is the sole monopoly source and creator of all money, who then is responsible for the blight of inflation? Who except the very institution that is solely empowered to create money, that is, the Fed (and the Bank of England, and the Bank of Italy, and other central banks) . . . ? In short . . . the Fed and the banks are not part of the solution to inflation. . . . In fact, they are the problem.[184]

By the 1990s, even the widely respected Paul Volcker, deemed one of the most successful of Fed chairmen, concluded that "By and large, if the overriding objective is price stability, we did a better job with the nineteenth century gold standard and passive central banks, with currency boards or even 'free banking'."[185]

As some economists see it, the economy not only had more stable prices before the creation of the Fed; it was more stable, period. Economist Gottfried Haberler observed that

During the second half of the nineteenth century there was a marked tendency for [economic] disturbances to become milder. Especially those conspicuous events, breakdowns, bankruptcies, and panics became less numerous, and there were even business cycles from which they were entirely absent. Before

[WWI], it was the general belief of economists that . . . dramatic breakdowns and panics . . . belonged definitely to the past.[186]

Milton Friedman has been even more critical:

The severity of each of the major contractions—1920–21, 1929–33, and 1937–38—is
directly attributable to acts of commission
and omission by the Reserve authorities and
would not have occurred under earlier monetary and banking arrangements.[187]

Free-market economists do not all agree about how
past economic contractions occurred. But all would
agree with Friedman's assertion that "The stock of
money, prices and output was decidedly more unstable after the establishment of the Reserve System than
before."[188]

Argument 3: Price-fixing is especially toxic for an economy, and central banks are basically price-fixers.

As we have previously noted, interest rates represent
the price of money, or technically the price of credit.
The price of credit in turn is really the price paid for
time, for deferring consumption from the present into
the future. That is, if I lend you money, I am putting
off my own immediate consumption. Once you pay
me back, I can spend my money, but not for the time
period covered by the loan. Since money and time are

involved in virtually every transaction in the economy, there is no more crucial price than the price for credit. Nineteenth-century economist Jean-Baptiste Say was right to say that "[The] rate of interest ought no more to be restricted, or determined by law, than ... the price of wine, linen, or any other commodity."[189]

But it is important to emphasize that restricting this particular price is especially dangerous, because the economy depends on free prices for information, and on this price more than any other.

Economic writer Gene Epstein has correctly stated that "[The Chairman of the Federal Reserve] is the head price fixer of a price-fixing agency."[190]

The agency not only fixes the short-term cost of credit, which in turn influences other interest rates. In addition, it heavily influences what is perhaps the second most important economic price, that of the U.S. dollar in world markets.

Moreover, this is a form of price-fixing whose deleterious effects are notoriously difficult to detect. As economic writer Gene Callahan explains:

> Because [interest rates are paid over] ... time, the negative effects of the artificial [credit] price take time to appear.... And because of that time lag, it is harder to trace the later problems to the earlier intervention."[191]

Argument 4: Central banks are national economic planners, and national economic planning does not work.

Like the debate about price controls, there is an ebb and flow to the perennial debate about economic planning. Adam Smith wrote at the end of the eighteenth century that:

> The statesman, who should attempt to direct private people in what manner they ought to employ their capitals, would not only load himself with a most unnecessary attention, but assume an authority which could safely be trusted, not only to no single person, but to no council or senate whatever, and which would nowhere be so dangerous as in the hands of a man who had folly and presumption enough to fancy himself fit to exercise it.[192]

For a considerable time, Smith's view prevailed, only to be superceded by Keynes's ideas and by what Barbara Wootton called in 1935 "The Necessity of Planning":

> There should be some body of nation-wide authority charged with the duty of constructing [an] ... economic ... plan for the whole country, or at least with the duty of reviewing all our partial plans—plans for housing, plans for the relief of distressed areas, agricultural

marketing plans, and so on—so as to make sure that they fit together.[193]

By the time the Berlin Wall fell in 1989 and Communism collapsed in the Soviet Union and elsewhere, the pendulum appeared to swing again. Economist Robert Heilbroner, a prominent friend of national economic planning, wrote in that same year:

> The contest between capitalism and socialism is over: capitalism has won. [We now have] . . . the clearest possible proof that capitalism organizes the material affairs of humankind more satisfactorily than socialism.[194]

Some years later in 1997, *The Economist* agreed that "Almost any discussion of public policy nowadays seems to begin and end with the same idea: the state is in retreat."[195] And economic historian David Landes added that "[All] sides blithely assume that free markets are in the saddle and riding the world."[196]

But was this assumption valid? Throughout the 1990s, central banks throughout the world were tightening their control of interest rates and currencies and taking on even more responsibility for guiding capital markets and economies. As economic writer James Grant observed:

> Central planning may be discredited in the broader sense, but people still believe in central planning as it is practiced by . . . [The U.S.

Federal Reserve]. . . . To my mind the Fed is a cross between the late, unlamented Interstate Commerce Commission and the Wizard of Oz. It is a Progressive Era regulatory body that, uniquely among the institutions of that era, still stands with its aura and prestige intact.[197]

Economist William Anderson agreed about the "aura," but was even more sharply critical:

Central banking, for all its "aura," is no less socialistic than the Soviet Union's Gosplan [the Soviet agency charged with creating Communist Russia's economic plan].[198]

The growing power and prestige of central banking was surprising in other ways as well. Throughout the 1990s, the Fed published its own forecasts of economic growth, usually expressed as a rather broad range. But a study of sixty quarters through year-end 2004 revealed that actual growth had fallen within the range only a quarter of the time.[199] The Fed, like a majority of economists, has never correctly forecast a recession.[200]

Gene Callahan has compared the Fed to a hyperactive pediatrician determined to intervene to ensure that a child under his or her care is growing at the "right rate."[201] In reality, no doctor, and no Fed chairman, can be sure what the "right" rate is, and interventions are little better than stabs in the dark.

Argument 5: The way that central banks operate, in particular the reliance on exceedingly flimsy tools and rules, is not reassuring.

The most famous rule for guiding monetary policy was Milton Friedman's: just pick a money supply growth rate and expand or contract the money supply to meet the target. This was an attempt to take discretionary decision-making away from unreliable central bankers, but proved impractical because the money supply could not be precisely defined, much less tracked, especially in a global economy. Another much cited rule developed by economist John Taylor of Stanford University also utilizes variables (e.g., potential output, inflation rate) that are hard to define or observe, and thus subject to endless debate and disagreement.[202]

These and many other formulas used by Fed and other monetary economists bring to mind a story told by social philosopher Irving Kristol about a friend's mother. The friend, who eventually became a leading novelist, used to bring college friends home to his family's New York City apartment for endless political debates. It was the 1930s, everyone was some stripe of Marxist, and the finer points of Marxist doctrine were argued into the night. The friend's mother, a Jewish immigrant without much formal schooling, hovered wordlessly and provided tray after tray of food and drink. Then:

Late one night, after they had all left, she turned to her son and said: Your friends— what brilliant young people! Smart! Smart!— and then, with a downward and dismissive sweep of her arm—Stupid.[203]

The thought that the world's monetary policy is worked out through discussions and equations vaguely reminiscent of what went on in that 1930s living room is not reassuring. How then do the monetary authorities get away with it, get away with taking so much decision-making away from the market with so little intellectual basis to what they do? One explanation is that easy money policies generally suit whatever party is in power, whether ostensibly of the left or the right, and central bank chairmen want to be reappointed.

Another, equally cynical, explanation has been offered by Milton Friedman:

[The Federal Reserve] System . . . blames all problems on external influences beyond its control and takes credit for any and all favorable occurrences. It thereby continues to promote the myth that the private economy is unstable, while its behavior continues to document the reality that government is today the major source of economic instability.[204]

Argument 6: The Greenspan Fed represents a case study in how an overactive central bank can create unintended consequences—without people understanding what has actually happened.

On the surface, Fed policies under the chairmanship of Alan Greenspan during the late 1980s, 1990s, and early 2000s seemed to work well: the economy boomed, the years stretched on without a recession, inflation (as measured by the consumer price index) remained largely dormant. But under the surface all was not well. A sharp increase in the U.S. money supply engineered by the Fed led to excessive corporate borrowing, much of which found its way into corporate stock repurchases (companies buying back their own stock), which fueled a stock market bubble, which inflated consumer spending and other bubbles. Greenspan seemed to pour fuel on the speculative fires by bailing out profligately overspending and overborrowing financial institutions and countries, intervening with sometimes dramatically timed interest rate cuts whenever stock prices softened, and preaching that technology had created a "new economic era."

After the 1990s bubble burst, corporations were so saddled with unproductive debt that their borrowing and investing had to be sharply curtailed. This would normally have led to a serious recession. Greenspan responded by cutting Fed interest rates to only 1% (less than the then-current inflation rate) in order to lure consumers into a similar overborrowing binge, and even counseled them in a celebrated speech to abandon the safety of fixed-rate home mortgages in favor of far riskier variable-rate mortgages. After this performance, Loews Corp CEO James Tisch only half-jokingly referred to the chairman of the Federal Reserve as "the Minister of National Speculation."[205]

As consumers responded to almost unprecedently easy money by borrowing and spending more, many of their purchases and much of the money they borrowed came from abroad. This had several negative consequences. In the first place, consumer purchasing power was drained out of the country by a growing trade and current account deficit and thereby created foreign, not U.S. jobs.

In the second place, the money borrowed from abroad was mostly being spent, not placed in productive, long-term investments. Because the U.S. chose to spend rather than invest much of its foreign borrowing, the interest was piling up without creating the wherewithal to pay it back. The U.S. had in effect become addicted to easy Japanese and then Chinese money. When it stopped, as it eventually would, U.S. interest rates would rise, consumer spending would fall, home and stock prices would also fall, as Paul Krugman and other economists predicted.[206] In the end, this could lead to waves of bankruptcy. For the moment, Americans felt secure and rich, just as the

Spanish felt secure and rich after they captured the gold of the Aztecs and Incas. But unless Americans recommitted themselves to the right path of working, saving, and investing, they would become, as the Spaniards became, "new poor."

The U.S. Federal Reserve has charge of American money, directly at home and indirectly abroad. But it also has charge of U.S. financial institutions, directly in the case of banks and indirectly in the case of other lenders. During Greenspan's tenure, the activities and balance sheets of banks changed radically, most dramatically in the issuance and trading of derivative securities such as financial futures and options. In 1990, the national value of all derivatives held by U.S. commercial banks was about $6 trillion; by 2004 this had exploded to almost $80 trillion[207] or almost seven times the value of U.S. annual output. Greenspan, speaking in his role as a bank regulator, testified that this proliferation of highly leveraged and little understood financial instruments was good for the health of the economy. Others wondered whether banks were not getting in over their heads and potentially jeopardizing themselves and the economy.

Looking back at the record of the Greenspan Fed, economist Marc Faber concluded that the concatenation of so many misjudgments and policy errors would eventually lead to demands for the dethronement of central bankers as national economic planners:

If monetary policies and central-bank interventions in the market economy should now fail—as I believe they will—the economic textbooks of the post Second World War period ... will have to be rewritten. I would also expect the power of central banks to be significantly curtailed.... When ... the public ... finally realizes that central bankers are no wiser than the central planners of former communist regimes, the tide will turn and monetary reform will come to the fore.... At that time ... market forces [will again] drive economic activity, and not some kind of central planner: regardless whether they stand forth as senior officials of totalitarian regimes—or come cleverly disguised as central bankers.[208]

Argument 7: Central banking represents a moral, not just a practical, problem.

Economist John Maynard Keynes spent most of his lifetime mocking the values of ordinary, middle-class people. It is not surprising that his economic theories, the theories that underlie modern central banking, turn the old copybook maxims of morality on their head. In the Keynesian world, technical cleverness matters more than hard work, spending is a virtue, saving is almost an anti-social act. People will be willful, capricious, subject to emotional extremes. But a wise government, staffed by people with the right kind of technical expertise, will guide the masses in the right direction, and will, if necessary, resort to a bit of seduction or mendacity to achieve necessary ends.

In the following passage, Keynes discusses how greedy and befuddled people are, but how they can be gulled through the device of a central bank:

> Unemployment develops, that is to say, because people want the moon [i.e., want their wages to be uneconomically high].... There is no remedy but to persuade the public that green cheese is practically the same thing [as money] and to have a green cheese factory (i.e., a central bank) under public control.[209]

Keynes has now passed from the scene, but his less nimble and witty heirs still run the central banks. The amount of debt that governments, businesses, or consumers take on, they all chorus together, is a purely technical matter. It has nothing to do with morality. Spending and even borrowing in order to spend is good for employment. Leave it to the experts, working stealthily behind closed central bank doors, to ensure that we get neither too much nor too little, but just the right amount. People who criticize all this—who, along with Paul Kasriel, chief economist for the Northern Trust Company, say that central banks are little more than "legal counterfeiters,"[210] that societies must save in order to become wealthy, that heavily indebted consumers are on a treadmill that will keep them poor forever—these people are just out-of-date.

Argument 8: Central banking serves the interests of politicians primarily, rich people secondarily, and the poor not at all.

Does central banking better serve the interests of the rich or the poor? This particular debate is a very old one, and can be traced to the beginning of the United States. The conventional wisdom, embodied in most history texts, records that Alexander Hamilton, secretary of the treasury under George Washington, correctly perceived the need for a central bank to guide the infant republic's economy. Unfortunately, President Thomas Jefferson displayed an ignorant antipathy toward banks, especially central banks, and his congressional followers succeeded in shutting down the first Bank of the United States in 1811. A second Bank of the United States was established in 1817, but Jefferson's even more radical heir Andrew Jackson closed it in 1836. Thereafter, the banking system and economy drifted through unnecessary crises until the Federal Reserve Act of 1913.

There are a number of flaws to this oft-told tale. First of all, Hamilton did want a central bank, but he specifically warned against governments or central banks printing paper money, as they do today:

> The emitting of paper money by the authority
> of Government is wisely prohibited....

> Though paper emissions, under a general authority, might have some advantage . . . yet they are of a nature so liable to abuse—and it may even be affirmed, so certain of being abused—that the wisdom of the Government will be shown in never trusting itself with the use of so seducing and dangerous an expedient. . . . The stamping of paper is an operation so much easier than the laying of taxes, that a government, in the practice of paper emissions, would rarely fail . . . to indulge itself too far in the employment of that resource. . . . even to [the point of creating] . . . an absolute bubble.[211]

Hamilton did not object to private banks issuing notes that were the equivalent of paper money. That was different, because it could be regulated by market forces. If a private bank overdid it: "It will return upon the bank."[212]

It is a complete mischaracterization of Jefferson and Jackson to say that they opposed banks, business, or modernity itself. What they especially feared, and with much justification, was that central banks would become the tools of politicians and their rich supporters. As Jackson said, "The mischief [in a central bank] springs from the power which the moneyed interest derives from a paper currency which they are able to control."[213]

When the Federal Reserve Act of 1913 came up for congressional consideration, Senator Elihu Root argued that Hamilton's and Jackson's words should be heeded. If a central bank were needed, it should at least be barred from issuing paper money. But most of Root's colleagues thought this precaution needless, since under the original legislation any paper money would be backed by and exchangeable into gold. How surprised they would all be to see that paper money is now backed by nothing at all.

In any case, the Fed did come into being, and the question remains: has it helped the poor? Again, the conventional wisdom would argue that it has, that an expanding money supply helps the economy grow, which helps the poor. This is the point of view of Alan Blinder, a former Fed vice chairman under President Clinton who has always focused on reducing income inequality. He argues that even if an expanding money supply brings with it some inflation, "The harm [which] inflation inflicts on the economy is often exaggerated."[214]

But is this true, especially for the poor? The poor after all are not generally able to borrow the new funds made available by the Fed to banks. It is businesses, rich people, people with assets and good credit records who are able to tap into these funds and take advantage of lower, Fed-reduced interest rates. Although the poor are generally unable to borrow, they do have to buy, and inflation relentlessly drives up the cost of everything they need.

Domingo Cavallo, the Finance Minister of Argentina in the 1990s, argued that the poor are the most "punished" by inflation, and this has been substantiated by numerous studies. For example, David Dollar and Aart Kraay of the World Bank studied eighty countries and found that reducing inflation was one of the most effective ways of helping the poor.[215] Allowing mild deflation of the sort that naturally occurs in an unhampered free market would help even more, and would have no adverse consequences for those without debts. And of course the destabilization produced by the Fed's attempt to stabilize the economy ultimately cost the poor more dearly than anyone else.

Argument 9: Central banking can and should be replaced.

Defenders of central banking allege that there are no real alternatives to the present system. This is false. Among the better alternatives are either gold or private (free) banking without a central bank. These alternatives made sense to Alexander Hamilton and other financial sages of an earlier age, and we could return to both.

Private (free) banking could also be strengthened by tightening reserve requirements, perhaps even requiring 100% reserves against loans.§

In the meantime, simply monetizing gold as an alternative currency and allowing gold-based checking

---

§ See this book's companion volume, *How Much Money Does An Economy Need?* (forthcoming from Axios Press in January 2008) for a discussion of "fractional reserve" banking and its consequences.

accounts and interest-bearing deposits would represent a step in the right direction.

Part Eleven

Four
Economic Value
Systems

23

Competing
Economic Value Systems

"Equalitarianism"

WHEN PEOPLE EMBRACE equalitarianism, the philosophy of living on a complete share-and-share-alike basis, they generally know that the way forward will not be smooth. They will have to overcome many obstacles in attempting to realize their vision. But what counts most to them is the vision itself—of helping others, living unselfishly. These are appealing ideals, appealing even for most opponents of equalitarianism.

Life is complex, however, and in addition to the equalitarian system of values, there are other, competing economic value systems. At the risk of greatly oversimplifying, there are at least three alternatives which we shall call: "fraternalism," "reciprocalism," and "philanthropism." A brief sketch of each follows.

"Fraternalism"

This particular economic value system appears to date from the very beginning of human history, and incorporates a series of powerful ideals.

The first and most commanding ideal is one of community, a community that provides safety and security for each of its members, physical but also economic safety and security. This community, it should be emphasized, does not operate on an equalitarian principle of share and share alike. On the contrary, it divides its wealth in ways which can be extremely unequal, but nevertheless looks out for the poorest, weakest, or least intelligent members of society and maintains some kind of "safety net" for them.

The next ideal is one of order, since a community cannot function in chaos. Order in turn has three further correlates: stability, strong leadership, and authority because order cannot be maintained without them. The last ideal is power because insecurity and powerlessness are seen as twin evils, the former curable only by curing the latter, which in turn requires a disciplined and well-led community. Of course, complete security and power for one community may mean complete insecurity and powerlessness for another, which can lead to trouble, but this gets ahead of our story.

According to the logic of fraternalism, relying on the power principle also means that government, not markets, should have the final say over the production and division of wealth in the community. Markets may flourish, as they generally do under advanced fraternalism, but they should be closely guided and regulated. Fraternalist governments tend not to be doctrinaire about globalized markets and free trade, but rather support or restrict them based on a calculation of how it affects the national interest.

Fraternalism seems to reflect the most basic human wants and needs. Life is hard and dangerous. We need each other. So like all primates, we subordinate our selfish desires for pleasure and status sufficiently to come together, to form families, clans, and larger family analogue communities under the guidance of powerful leaders.

Both the ideals imbedded in fraternalism and the heroic actions that may be inspired by them have become the stuff of legend: ancient Spartans standing at Thermopylae, facing certain death, to defend Greece from Persian invaders; Horatio standing alone on a bridge of ancient Rome defying an entire enemy army; Churchill defying Hitler early in World War Two; a handful of almost unimaginably brave British airmen saving their nation from Nazi barbarism at the same time; everyday Americans feeding each other and lending a hand to each other during the devastation of the Great Depression; Japanese and Germans scrimping, saving, and working together to rebuild their economies from the ruins of World War Two, and so on throughout history.

As of this writing, fraternalist values are not only the foundation for others. They still largely dominate, in advanced economies including America's, Europe's and Japan's, as well as elsewhere in the world. The Democratic Party in the U.S. is largely fraternalist in orientation, but so is the Republican Party notwithstanding their differences, both real and rhetorical. And so it goes in most countries.

Fraternalist-inspired economic systems of the fifteenth through eighteenth centuries are sometimes referred to by historians as "mercantilist." Contemporary fraternalist systems are also sometimes called "neo-mercantilist," mostly by critics. A more sympathetic term to describe them might be "state-led capitalism."

"Reciprocalism"

As reciprocalists see it, the place to start in building an economic system is not with an ideal of huddling together for safety and security, nor with the related ideals of community, order, stability, directive leadership, authority, and power. Yes, we all need each other; no one can stand alone. But in order to foster the right kind of cooperation, the place to start is with an ideal of independence, of each economic player taking personal responsibility for himself or herself, doing his or her part, standing as far as possible on his or her own feet, not being an unnecessary burden on others, and thereby earning not only self-respect and good will, but also the communal assistance of others. The trouble with the family model writ larger and larger in fraternal social systems is that it feeds the grandiosity of parental leaders, bestows far too much power (with all its temptations) on them, and infantilizes everyone else.

Moreover, we are told, a philosophy of independence, personal responsibility, and reciprocal cooperation makes us happier. As naturalist and philosopher Alexander Skutch has written:

> If we remember that the stranger of whom we ask a direction owes nothing to us, his courteous response will be more appreciated and will lighten our steps if the journey is long. If we never expect anything of anybody, we

shall . . . be more grateful for everything that is done for us.[216]

Reciprocalism further teaches that:

- We serve ourselves best by serving others, for example by producing the finest goods we can make and honestly exchanging them for those of others;

- Exchanging is healthier than giving, because neither giving nor taking are healthy if isolated from each other;*

- Competition is healthy if channeled into constructive projects for the betterment of humanity;

- Free economic markets are the right place for competition;

- Free global markets should be fostered and will reduce or someday even extinguish war;

- Pluralism is better than centralized, hierarchical leadership;

- Change should be welcomed, not resisted as socially destabilizing;

- Competing entrepreneurs, operating in free markets, are the essential agents of constructive change, economic growth and progress;

---

* This is evidently quite an old idea, since the ancient Indo-European root for the modern English word "giving" seems to have meant either giving or taking or both giving and taking, which suggests that early humans viewed these actions as being so closely related that a single word sufficed for both.

Knowledge and discovery are critical to successful entrepreneurship;

▓ People should not be protected from the consequences of their own choices or actions;

▓ Whenever people are protected from their own errors, mistakes accumulate instead of being liquidated, and economic growth grinds to a halt;

▓ Trust, honesty, decency, self-discipline, thrift, saving, and patience (what in the nineteenth century was called "character"), will eventually lead us, through the power of compounding, out of poverty and deprivation.

Laissez-faire, the economic and social system in which reciprocalist ideas of "independence first, then cooperation," are most boldly expressed, has been called cold, heartless, soulless, unethical (or alternatively machine-like and thus non-ethical), greedy, exploitative, war-mongering, mean, materialistic, etc. But a fair reading of the larger reciprocalist philosophy is that it is loaded with ideals, just different ideals than are to be found in fraternalism, and that both are due at least a respectful hearing.

"Philanthropism"

Charity is an ancient ideal, one with the explicit authority of the New Testament:

> Then shall [the king of heaven] say unto
> them on the left hand . . . I was hungry, and
> you gave me no food. I was thirsty, and you
> gave me no drink. I was a stranger, and you
> took me not in. Naked, and you clothed me
> not. Sick, and in prison, and you visited me
> not. . . . And these shall go away into everlast-
> ing punishment.[217]

Although the concept of charity seems ingrained in us, it is not without its critics. Again, the naturalist and philosopher Alexander Skutch:

> In an ideal society, universal friendly coop-
> eration [i.e., the kind of friendly coopera-
> tion defined by reciprocalism] would prevail,
> but material charity would be rare. . . . Alms-
> giving fosters feelings of inadequacy and
> dependence, and is as likely to generate envy
> as gratitude. Nature provides many examples
> of cooperation among organisms of the same
> or different species, but few that resemble
> almsgiving.[218]

When people undertake private acts of charity, we tend to think of this in moral rather than economic terms. But charity inevitably begets and becomes embodied in charitable institutions. Especially in the United States, such institutions (often referred to as the not-for-profit or non-profit sector) represent a separate and complementary economic system—a system that is distinguishable, on the one hand, from the world of private ownership and, on the other hand, from the world of government. In effect, non-profits embody an alternative vision, as well as an economic and social system, one that could play an even more meaningful role than it does.

In summary, we have now identified four alternative economic value systems:

FRATERNALISM. These values reflect our tribal origins and provide a foundation for all economic arrangements. Among the most important fraternalist ideals are: community, safety and security, order, stability, leadership, authority, and power.

RECIPROCALISM. These values have always been with us, but came to particular prominence as an eighteenth-century protest and reform movement aimed at correcting the alleged defects of fraternalism, especially government predation and corruption. Among the most important reciprocalist ideals are: independence, personal responsibility, reciprocal cooperation, openness to change, and indirectly, a limited role for government in the economy.

EQUALITARIANISM. These values are equally ancient, and also gathered force as a protest and reform movement, this time as a nineteenth-century protest against the reciprocalist acceptance and even promotion of human inequality. The contrary ideal of complete economic equality is compatible with either strong centralized government control or, alternatively, no government role at all.

PHILANTHROPISM. These values—of charity, altruism, and service—have been approved, to a greater or lesser extent, by every known human society, and are especially recommended by all leading world religions. Yet even they have their critics. Some charge that charity degrades the receiver and creates dependency. Others charge that philanthropists are Pharisees, hypocrites, egoists, even surreptitious power mongers.

In differentiating these value systems, it is important to remember that all of them may claim a specific ideal for its own. But, if so, they will usually define, interpret, or rank it differently. Thus, reciprocalists will insist that they too believe in equality, albeit an equality of opportunity rather than outcome. They may also extol charity, although a strict application of the principle of reciprocity would seem to forbid it. And so it goes, with words being continually redefined and reinterpreted and values being traded off one against another.

The broader issues raised by the four alternative economic value systems are as old as human beings, or indeed as old as higher primates. Long-term studies of chimpanzees, for example by Jane Goodall in the wild or by Frans de Waal in more closely observed captive settings, suggest that any group of primates must make choices between independence and community, stability and change, social power and reciprocal cooperation, and so forth. The choices that individual primates or groups of primates make are quite eclectic, often inconsistent, as well as inconstant.

As human beings, we operate on a higher plane. Our choices often take the form of ideas, even of ideals, as we have emphasized. But, in true primatological fashion, we prefer not to choose among our different ideals; we want to have everything. In the end, we choose between alternatives because we have to, because life will not simultaneously give us both complete independence and a warm feeling of community. Moreover, we may further complicate or confuse matters by deceiving ourselves or others about we want or believe, by failing to live up to what we believe, by forming temporary alliances with others through the expedient of glossing over or ignoring differences in what we want or believe, or simply by changing our mind.

Whatever the twists and turns of the human valuation process, we are always confronted with some fundamental economic questions, questions that cannot be evaded, that must be answered and answered anew in each generation.

So far in this book, we have offered many answers, but none of our own. We will now deviate from this course a little by looking more deeply into what we have called philanthropism, and by suggesting that an expansion of philanthropic values along with the non-profit economic sector might conceivably help bring together equalitarians, fraternalists, and reciprocalists, heal some of the battle wounds, and foster more of the economic cooperation that almost everyone wants.

Part Twelve

Reconciling Opposing Viewpoints

24

Expanding the Non-Profit Sector

W**HY WOULD AN EXPANSION** of the non-profit sector potentially help bring economic antagonists together, heal wounds, and foster economic cooperation? To see why this might be so, we must begin with contemporary equalitarians. As noted previously, they are of two minds about how best to end economic inequality, some favoring persuasion, others favoring draconian government programs to reallocate wealth. But, despite this difference, most agree that "progressive" taxation, that is, subjecting the wealthy not only to higher taxes, but to higher tax rates on income and estates, is the only decent way for government to raise its revenue.

Fraternalists do not embrace the idea of equality per se. But they do embrace "progressive" taxation for reasons of their own. In the first place, extremes of wealth are thought to undermine a sense of community, an all-important value for fraternalists. In the second place, a real community should have a social "safety net" for the poorest and most disadvantaged, and heavier taxation if the rich can help fund this. In the third place, fraternalist politicians know that they need equalitarian voters to reach a majority, and that appeals for heavier taxation will help bring in these voters. The fraternalist/equalitarian electoral alliance has been successful all over the world, and very few democracies have not embraced the basic goal of reallocated wealth to at least some degree through the tax system.

Reciprocalists remain the lone dissenters from all this. "Progressive" taxation, they say, merely swells the size of government without actually reallocating wealth to the less advantaged. Most of the extra money raised from the rich does not reach the poor—indeed in a majority of developed democracies, including the U.S., government subsidies for the well-off considerably exceed subsidies for the poor. Moreover, heavy taxation of the rich dissipates society's savings, actual or potential, which reduces economic growth, and harms the poor most of all. All things considered, Reciprocalists believe that a "flat" tax is best, even if social "safety nets" have to be reduced as a result.

We need not revisit these quarrels, except to note

that "progressive" and "flat" taxes, as conventionally conceived, do not exhaust all the possibilities. Another alternative is to keep "progressive" taxes, but to use them, not to expand government, but rather to expand the non-profit sector of the economy.

At the present time the non-profit sector represents about 8% of the U.S. economy, and considerably less elsewhere.[219] The question we will now address is whether this sector could play a larger role in the U.S. and elsewhere, especially in social services for the poor and disadvantaged, but also in healthcare, education, and other critical areas.

One obvious way to expand the non-profit sector is to increase government funding. It is estimated that the one hundred largest U.S. charities already receive over 20% of their income from the government.[220] With the model of government funding already well established, these numbers could rise dramatically. As political columnist Joe Klein has said about Andrew Cuomo, the secretary of housing under President Clinton:

> "Andrew Cuomo is a guy with [a] ... brilliant ... idea: Government cannot provide social services. The best thing for government to do is to provide a check to the altruistic people who should provide services and who have the flexibility to change their programs on a dime."[221]

This notion also has its critics, however. They cite one or more of the following objections:

❚❚ If government funding increases, charities will lose both their independence and their flexibility.

❚❚ Government funding blows with the political winds, and will never be a reliable source of support.

❚❚ Present quarrels over whether government should fund religious charities (Republicans for, Democrats against) will only intensify.

❚❚ Government subsidies always fail because they increase the demand for services without increasing the supply. The result is inflation, with soaring prices outrunning subsidies by a mile. This has already happened in medicine, housing, and education, with dire results for the poor especially. Why add anything else to this list?

❚❚ Charity should always represent an act of personal compassion. Redistribution of income and assets through progressive taxation represents a different act and the two should not be confused. No one fulfills a personal charitable obligation by paying taxes, no matter how heavily, and certainly no one fulfills that obligation by voting in favor of others paying higher taxes.

Direct government funding of charities is not, however, the only way that government could foster the growth of the charitable sector. Another way would be to revise the tax code. At the present time, donors to Internal Revenue Service–approved charities may deduct their gift. If I am in a 35% tax bracket, and deduct my gift from taxable income, that means the government in effect bears 35% of the cost of my gift. The gift still represents a personal sacrifice, because I bear 65% of the cost, but government is making it easier to give. Taking all aspects of the tax code into account, many wealthy people pay 50% or more in taxes and thus benefit from a comparable charitable deduction.

An alternative idea would be to convert a deduction (on taxable income) into a credit (on tax owed). This would leave the taxpayer with a simple choice: would I prefer my money to go to the government or to charity, since a credit would mean that the government is bearing the full cost.

Clearly, government could not afford to offer this choice unrestrictedly, since it could lead to a collapse of tax revenue. But, to begin with, the tax code could be revised to provide a credit for social service donations only, or for donations made from what would otherwise be taxes paid in the top tax brackets, or for donations made from what otherwise would have been estate taxes.

Providing a credit for social service donations would increase the flow of money to the poor and needy.

These funds could further supplement government support or gradually replace government support with the more "entrepreneurial," "flexible," and "cost-effective" private programs that Joe Klein and Andrew Cuomo want. Moreover, if it wished, the government could see how much money was being raised this way and adjust its own programs accordingly: more if donations are down, less if donations are up.

It will be objected that services would be less uniform this way. But social services already vary greatly in the U.S., because they are primarily administered by the individual states. Management by private charities could be more creative and responsive to the particular needs and character of the individual poor or needy person. If additional oversight and monitoring were desired, "credit-worthy" social services donations might have to go to grant-making foundations which would then pay it out to on-the-ground operating charities.

The idea of a social services tax credit is not new. Senator Dan Coats of Indiana proposed in 1996 a "poverty tax credit" of $500 for individuals and $1,000 for couples filing jointly, provided that the donation was made to organizations primarily working to help the poor and the disadvantaged.[222] Leading Republican pollster Frank Luntz thought that Coats was, as the *Washington Post* put it, "onto something big," a way to reframe and redirect the increasingly sterile debate about government social services.[223] The proposal sank without a trace. But some proponents thought that it failed by being too modest, too tentative in what it tried to accomplish.

A bolder proposal might look like this. Everyone in the U.S. would pay a simple income tax, with only a few permitted deductions (including ordinary charitable deductions), to support the operations of the government. The threshold income required to trigger the tax would be set high, so the poor would not pay income tax at all. Above the initial tax bracket used to fund the government, there would be one or at most two brackets more for the rich, however defined. The rich could either pay these additional taxes to the government or receive a full tax credit by donating the same amount to registered social service charities (or grant-making foundations required to pass the funds on to social services charities).

If this approach were adopted, the tax code would be vastly simplified; the system would still be "progressive" because the rich would still have to pay more; the government would set upper rates based on society's needs, not its own; and more support would reach the poor.

The last point is worth emphasizing. If one assumes that the larger purpose of progressive taxation is to redistribute income, to move income from the rich to the poor, this would be a more efficient way to accomplish that aim. It would be more efficient because, as previously noted, very little of upper-bracket tax money is actually flowing through to the needy. The greater portion by far is simply used by government for its ordinary expenses, including major subsidies for the rich and middle class.

There are other advantages to a system of charitable tax credits. One of the chief criticisms of progressive tax rates is that they curtail savings, especially the savings of new business owners. Established rich people and businesses already have savings to draw upon for investment. A rising entrepreneur may obtain income, but find that it takes years to save and accumulate capital from income, because so much is taken in taxes. This is a kind of hidden "subsidy" of the rich, one which to some degree protects their firms and investments from "new men and women" and "new business ideas." It also reduces the rate of overall capital formation and therefore of economic growth.

A way to address this issue would be to let entrepreneurs escape upper-bracket taxation if they saved and reinvested the savings, but with the investment gains required to be paid to charities. In effect, the entrepreneurs would have the use of the funds when they needed them for business purposes, but would gradually become partners with their own or others' charities. The likely mechanism would be for the entrepreneur to donate to a charity, but be able to stipulate that the gift will be reinvested (or simply remain in) the business in exchange for ownership.

Estate taxes, payable after a person's death, are a special case. The arguments in favor of them are that:

- The government needs the revenue;
- Large pools of private wealth should be discouraged;
- Unearned income is socially undesirable;
- Society has a right to redistribute the money to those in greater need;
- No one is harmed, because it is a tax on the dead, and the dead cannot be harmed.

The arguments against are that:

- The money has already been taxed in one way or another (including at the company level), often several times;
- The desire to leave money to one's children is instinctual and the right to do so is a powerful motivation to work, save, and build wealth;
- The money is already working hard meeting society's needs if it is invested;
- Taxing it means that a lifetime's savings, carefully nurtured by experienced investors, disappears overnight into the maw of government spending;
- Government's tendency to prey on and recklessly consume investment capital over the millennia is precisely what has kept the human race so poor.

These arguments will never be resolved, but they might be reconciled to a degree through an estate-tax credit for charity. If an entrepreneur were able to leave money to his or her own family charity, with assurance that family control would be maintained, the motivation to build fortunes would not be much compromised. If the capital could be donated and preserved as an endowment, the capital accumulation of a lifetime would be maintained, not dissipated, and the family would have good reason to want to keep tending and growing it from generation to generation.

But is it wise to use tax credits to build up the charitable sector in the U.S. and elsewhere? Columnist Ted Rall thinks that charitable givers are just "so many suckers [who]" let . . . lazy, incompetent and corrupt politicians off the hook" from their responsibilities to care for the disadvantaged with tax revenues. Rall continues: "We live in the United States, not Mali. . . . [Must] the sick, poor and unlucky . . . live and die at the whim of . . . charit[able] contributors[?]"[224]

There are many other possible objections as well. When charitable institutions grow and grow, they may become worlds unto themselves, rich but still money hungry, fat, self-satisfied, too quick to add or overpay staff, reward friends, build buildings. If a business corporation falls prey to these ills, the board of directors is supposed to demand change. If not, shareholders can replace both board and management, although the process may be expensive, difficult, or time-consuming. Charitable organizations have neither profit and loss statements nor shareholders, so accountability is difficult to achieve.

For some, the answer lies in more government regulation. At the present time, there is a great deal of U.S. regulation of charities, but little enforcement, because neither the Internal Revenue Service nor the states' attorneys general have much staff for the purpose. If tax credits diverted billions of new dollars to charities, no doubt both the amount of regulation and of regulatory staff would multiply, but this could be a very mixed blessing. It could make charities much more bureaucratic, much less flexible. It could make them look more and more like government itself.

There are many other possible objections to more government regulation of charities. In particular, it may be argued that much of the regulation already in place is seriously misguided. For example, at present self-dealing and other rules make it impossible for an entrepreneur to donate non-marketable shares in his or her own business to a charity. This is not wise, because more charitable ownership of business would be good for both charity and business. Perhaps even more seriously, charity law has increasingly assumed that "family" control of foundations and charities is undesirable. Numerous additional proposals, not yet enacted into law, would have virtually banned family control.

In reality, "private" control of charitable organizations has major benefits. As in businesses, it both motivates and provides skilled, focused, innovative managers, individuals who will search out pockets of opportunity overlooked by others or squeeze every bit of value out of a dollar. The alternative of so-called public (i.e., not individual or family) control is not a bad one; it may be the only alternative after the passing of a founder. But one must guard against "public" control becoming bureaucratic control, or control by a group of unproductive insiders, and new forms of accountability must be found. In particular, members of the general public might be given legal standing to challenge a charity that does not seem to be operating according to the rules.

In any case, whatever the current regulatory errors, whatever the risks, whatever the caveats, an expansion of philanthropic values (along with an expansion of the non-profit sector of the economy through tax credits) could offer a way forward out of the old, bitter, and often sterile economic quarrels of the past.

Appendices

Appendix A
What Is a "Fair" Price?

THE "COST" THEORY OF VALUE was originally formulated by laissez-faire proponents Adam Smith and David Ricardo. In essence, it holds that products are worth what they cost to produce. Karl Marx pointed out that, in this case, it is difficult to justify adding a profit margin.

The Marxist "labor theory of value" holds that the only true costs are labor costs, and that workers, not owners, should receive any "surplus value" created by selling a product for more than it cost in wages. In making this argument, Marx was not blind to the role of factories and machine tools (i.e., capital) in making products. But he considered capital to be simply embodied labor, previous labor that was now wrongfully controlled by capitalists.

Most economists eventually concluded that Smith and Ricardo were wrong to think that a product has an objective value, and also wrong to think that this objective value would be a function of cost. Economic value is subjective, not objective; it is in the eye of the buyer. A desk may cost $75 to make, but if no one wants it, it has a value of zero. Conversely, if many people want it, it may be worth much more than $75. It is precisely because I value the desk at $100, and you (who own the desk) value it at less than $100 that a mutually advantageous trade develops. If the desk had an objective value, and everyone agreed about it, there might never be a trade.

There are other inconsistencies specific to Marx. If capital is previous labor, why should current workers get all the profit from it? Why not the previous workers themselves (although they may be dead or, if not, impossible to locate)? Also, if people should be paid "according to their needs," as Marx says in passages unrelated to the labor theory,[225] why should workers profit even from their own work? And Marx never did explain how to divide the profits a'mong the workers, if they did receive them.[226]

Even if we accept the proposition that economic values are subjective, and therefore have no theoretical connection to cost, many of us will still feel that prices should not be too much higher than production cost. For example, according to this line of thought, a price that is twice as high as production cost would definitely be an "unfair" price and therefore represent price "gouging."

Free-market proponents respond that, when demand is strong, very high prices are helpful, because they will persuade producers to step up production and also attract new competitors into the industry. Additional production will then bring prices back down and, even better, may reduce unit production costs. If this analysis is correct, most prices over long periods of time should not exceed costs by a large amount. Of course, the idea that markets are reliably self-correcting in this way is much disputed.

Appendix B
What Exactly Are Profits?

EFINING WHAT PROFITS are, and estimating their size in a market economy, is no simple task. We might start with the problem represented by capital gains.

We often become aware of a person's wealth when he or she sells a company, sells shares in a company by taking it "public," or otherwise sells property. Assuming that the asset is sold for more than the purchase price, the rich person realizes a capital gain, sometimes a dramatic capital gain, and it is natural to think of capital gains as the larger part of rich peoples' income and the most important way that they realize profits. This assumption, however, is incorrect, as explained by economists Jay and David Levy:

> Capital gains are not profits. . . . When one
> investor sells property to another inves-
> tor . . . [,] they merely exchange property. One
> gives the other money and gets a work of art,
> securities, or other assets. The net holdings of
> the 'investor class' are unchanged![227]

This requires some reflection. If capital gains are not profits, they are still linked to profits. We often realize a capital gain by selling our right to a future stream of profits, as for example when we sell a stock. Also we may increase our capital gain if we sell at a time when the economy is booming and profits are generally high. But the Levys are right to caution us. It is commonplace to say that a company chief executive officer "made" $15 million in a given year. On closer inspection, it becomes apparent that most of the money came from the sale of stock or options that had been held for much longer than the year in question and that represented the net present value of a stream of profits expected to continue far into the future.

There is also legitimate debate about whether the interest from loans or bonds that rich people receive should be counted as profits. This is another complicated issue that may depend in part on the type of bonds we are talking about. For example low-quality corporate bonds issued by companies as an equity substitute are different than high-quality bonds. On balance, it seems simpler and defensible to include all business interest payments as well as stock dividends when trying to calculate what investors actually receive in profits.

It is common for economic textbooks to discuss profits in general by focusing on "corporate" profits. The first point to be noted about "corporate" profits is that they refer only to so-called "C" corporations, which are subject to the corporate income tax, and not to sole proprietorships, partnerships, "S" corporations, limited liability companies, and business trusts, all of which are subject to personal rather than corporate taxes. Owners of these "non-C-corporate" businesses have a great deal of flexibility about whether they pay themselves a salary and, if so, whether it is a "market" level salary. Consequently, their business income may or may not represent true profit, which should be net of the fair value of their labor.

When looking strictly at "C corporation" profits, one should also ask whether the figures are net of losses, net of taxes, and adjusted for inflation. Corporate profits were negative at the bottom of the Great Depression, then reached a high of 15% of gross domestic product coming out of World War Two; but that was pre-tax, and corporate taxes were over 50% at the time, so the tax adjusted figure was closer to 7%.

Appendix C

Did the U.S. Congress Trigger the Stock Market Bubble of the Late 1990s?

A NUMBER OF CONGRESSIONAL actions may have contributed to the U.S. stock market and economic bubble of the late 1990s. For example, a law passed in the early 1990s limited the cash compensation of leaders of public companies. This shifted more and more executive compensation to stock options and thus may have inadvertently encouraged stock speculation. The accounting profession's policy board was also warned by leading senators that if it persisted in a plan to require companies to treat stock options as ordinary business expenses, legislation would put a stop to it. The policy board chose to bow before congressional pressure.

Tax laws throughout these years permitted companies to deduct the cost of borrowing money, but treated dividend payments to shareholders as taxable twice, once at the company level and again at the shareholder level. This made equity financing much more expensive than debt financing, and thus encouraged companies to borrow heavily. In part, companies borrowed heavily to buy back shares, a move that sent share prices higher and higher and (not incidentally) made the value of company executives' stock options soar. Meanwhile, prominent financial experts such as Franco Modigliani and Merton Miller were encouraging companies to incur more and more debt, on the assumption that debt and equity were interchangeable, that the risks of leverage were not as great as previously supposed. It may have been good theory, but dangerous theory for companies that edged too close to insolvency.[228]

Other tax laws required companies selling capital goods to book their earnings all at once, but permitted companies buying the capital goods to recognize the expense over a number of years. This treatment exaggerates reported corporate profits during a boom, when capital goods are most in demand, then exaggerates the decline in profits after the bust, when the sellers have few orders and the buyers are still expensing the purchases of prior years, many of which will have turned out to be mistakes.

The U.S. Federal Reserve probably had more impact on the U.S. economy than Congress in the late 1990s, but Congress also arguably played an important role.

Notes

Part One: The Central Economic Problem

Chapter 1: Why Are We Still So Poor?

1 Milton Friedman, *Essays in Positive Economics* (Chicago: The University of Chicago Press, 1970), 4.

Part Two: The Rich

Chapter 4: Are the Rich Necessary?—No

2 Howard Baetjer Jr., *Free To Try* (Irvington-on-Hudson: The Foundation for Economic Education, 1995), 103. Baetjer subsequently changed his assessment of Mr. Phelps.

3 *Newsweek* (November 9 1981): 108.

4 P. J. Proudhon, *What is Property* (1840).

5 Isaiah 3:14–15; also in S. Jay Levy and David Levy, *Profits and the Future of American Society* (New York: Mentor Books, 1984), 11.

6 George Gilder, *Wealth and Poverty* (Toronto: Bantam Books, 1981), 122.

7 Quoted by Malcolm Deas, "Catholics and Marxists," in *London Review of Books* (March 19, 1981); also in P. T. Bauer, *Reality and Rhetoric: Studies in the Economics of Development* (Cambridge, MA: Harvard University Press, 1984), 79.

8 Julius Nyerere, *The Economic Challenge* (London: 1976); also in *Reality and Rhetoric*, 79.

9 *The Free Market* (March 2003): 5.

Chapter 5: Are the Rich Necessary?—Yes

10 Wilhelm Röpke, *Economics of the Free Society* (Chicago: Henry Regnery Company, 1963), 10.

11 Paul Johnson, *Forbes* (April 14, 2003): 43.

12 Henry Hazlitt, *The Failure of "New Economics": An Analysis of the Keynesian Fallacies* (New Rochelle, NY: Arlington House, 1978), 246.

13 Henry Hazlitt, *The Conquest of Poverty* (Irvington-on-Hudson, NY: The Foundation for Economic Education, 1994), 227–28.

14 Ibid, p. 234.

15 Ibid, p. 228.

16 A.P. news story, *Yahoo News*, May 11, 2003.

17 Irving Kristol, *The Wall St. Journal* (June 26, 1979): Op Ed.

18 Thomas Sowell, *Forbes* (January 30, 1995): 81.

Part Three: The Rich in a Democracy

Chapter 6: Are the Rich Compatible with Democracy? —No

19 *C-ville Weekly* (October 8–14, 2002): 14.

20 *Pimco Fed Focus* (August 2004): 2.

Chapter 7: Are the Rich Compatible with Democracy? —Yes

21 Edwin Cannan, *An Economist's Protest* (New York: Adelphi Company, 1928), 429.

22 Ludwig von Mises, *Economic Policy: Thoughts for Today and Tomorrow* (Lake Bluff, IL: Regnery Gateway, 1985), 20.

23 Ibid.

24 Ibid., 1.

25 Ludwig von Mises, *Human Action: A Treatise On Economics* (Chicago: Henry Regnery Co., 1966); also in Gene Callahan, *Economics for Real People: An Introduction to the Austrian School* (Auburn, AL: The Ludwig von Mises Institute, 2002), 298.

26 Abba Lerner, Everybody's Business (Lansing, MI: Michigan State University Press, 1961), 98.

27 Röpke, *Against the Tide* (Chicago: Henry Regnery Company, 1969), 38.

28 Ropke, *Economics of the Free Society*, 11.

29 Mises, *Human Action*, 684, also in Hazlitt, *Conquest of Poverty*, 214.

30 *Forbes* (October 6, 2003): 60.

31 *Forbes* (October 11, 2004): 52.

32 *The New York Times* (July 20, 1992): D–1; and *Forbes*, (April 21, 1997): 112.

Part Four: Profit-making

Chapter 8: Are Private Profits Necessary?—No

33 Ted Honderich, *After the Terror* (Edinburgh, 2002), 137–38; cited in *The Mises Review* 9, no. 1 (Spring 2003): 15–16.

34 Howard Zinn, emeritus professor of History, Boston

University and author of american history texts and other books, Internet interview by David Barsamion, Boulder, CO, Nov. 11, 1992.

35 *Weekly Standard* (December 8, 2003): 20.

36 Cynthia Tucker, Op. Ed, *Atlanta Journal—Constitution*, Yahoo News, June 24, 2004.

Chapter 9: Are Private Profits Necessary—Yes

37 Mark Kurlansky, *Cod* (New York: Vintage Books, 2004), cited in *Marathon Global Investment Review* (Aug 31, 2004): 2.

38 Karl Marx and Friedrich Engels, *The Communist Party Manifesto* (1848).

39 Mises, *Human Action*, 721.

40 Henry Hazlitt, *The Wisdom of Henry Hazlitt* (Irvington-on-Hudson: The Foundation for Economic Education, 1993), 86.

41 Lester Brown press release, November 6, 2001.

42 *The Free Market* (January 2003), 1.

43 Wilhelm Röpke, *Economics of the Free Society*, 235.

44 See, for example, Rhys Isaac, *Landon Carter's Uneasy Kingdom* (Oxford: Oxford University Press, 2004).

45 Mises, *Economic Policy*, 3.

46 Milton Friedman, *Capitalism and Freedom* (Chicago: University of Chicago Press, 1962), 170.

47 Milton and Rose Friedman, *Free to Choose: A Personal Statement* (New York: Avon Books, 1981), 138.

48 For a helpful account of all these convoluted relationships, see Levy, *Profits and the Future*, especially chap. 3, p. 20.

49 See, for example, Frances Moore Lappé, *The Quickening of America: Rebuilding Our Nation, Remaking Our Lives* (San Francisco: Jossey-Bass, Inc., 1944), 90.

50 *The Economist* (September 28, 1996): 28.

Chapter 10: Are Private Profits Necessary?—No/Yes

51 A term coined by Michael Polanyi (1951); also see Sanford Ikeda, *Dynamics of the Mixed Economy*: Toward
a theory of interventionism (London and New York:
Routledge, 1997), 256 passim.

52 Friedrich Hayek, "The Use of Knowledge in Society,"
American Economic Review 35:4 (September 1945):
519–30. Reprinted in *Individualism and Economic
Order* (Chicago: Henry Regnery, 1972), 77–91.

53 Paul Johnson, in *Will Capitalism Survive* (Washington, DC, 1979), 4; also in Michael Novak, *The Spirit
of Democratic Capitalism* (New York: Madison Books,
1982), 121.

Part Five: Profit-making and Depressions

**Chapter 11: Does the Profit System Cause Depressions?
—Yes/No**

54 Walter Lippmann, *Interpretations: 1931–1932* (New
York: Macmillan Company, 1932), 38.

55 *Washington Post* (April 29, 1993): A–22.

56 George Soros, *The Crisis of Global Capitalism: Open
Society Endangered* (New York: PublicAffairs Books,
1998); also quoted in Brink Lindsey, *Against the Dead
Hand*: The Uncertain Struggle for Global Capitalism
(New York: John Wiley & Sons, Inc., 2002), 190.

57 Jay Jasinowski, ed., *The Rising Tide: The Leading Minds
of Business and Economics Chart a Course Toward
Higher Growth and Prosperity* (New York: John Wiley
& Sons, Inc., 1998), xxvii.

58 Walter Lippman, *The Method of Freedom* (New York:
Macmillan Company, 1934), 58–59.

59　Lippmann, *Interpretations*, 103–105.

60　Friedrich Hayek, *Business Week* (December 15, 1980): 110.

61　Röpke, *Economics of the Free Society*, 219; also in Randall Holcombe, *15 Great Austrian Economists* (Auburn, AL: Ludwig von Mises Institute, 1999), 215.

62　Krugman, *Peddling Prosperity* (New York: W. W. Norton & Company, 1994), 32.

63　Friedrich A. Hayek, *Monetary Theory and the Trade Cycle* (London: Jonathan Cape Ltd., 1933), 21–22.

Part Six: The Global Profit System

Chapter 12: Does Global Free Trade Destroy Jobs?—Yes

64　Lawrence Summers, Godkin Lecture, Kennedy School of Government, Harvard University, 2003, quoted in *Harvard Magazine* (July/August 2003): 75.

65　Jerry Flint, *Forbes* (June 6, 2005): 174.

66　Peter Lynch, *Barrons* (January 26, 1987): 16.

67　William Greider, *One World, Ready or Not: The Manic Logic of Global Capitalism* (New York: Simon & Schuster, 1997), 25.

68　Al Sharpton, *The New York Times* (September 26, 2003): A–21.

69　A. Schlesinger, Jr., *Foreign Affairs* 76, no. 5 (September/October 1997): 8; also in Lindsey, *Against the Dead Hand*, 5.

70　R. Gephardt, *The Washington Post* (January 15, 2004): A–8.

71　Episode Three, *The Commanding Heights*, Public Broadcast Corporation.

Chapter 13: Does Global Free Trade Destroy Jobs?—No

72 To check the math, see Thomas Sowell, *Basic Economics: A Citizen's Guide to the Economy* (New York: Basic Books, 2000), 272–74.

73 *Forbes* (September 20, 2004): 43; citing study by Global Insight (USA).

74 Gene Epstein, *Barrons* (November 17, 2003).

75 L. Rockwell, *The Free Market* (October 2003): 6.

76 Jagdish Bhagwati, Geoffrey Wood, ed., *Explorations in Economic Liberalism: The Wincott Lectures* (London: Macmillan, 1996), 194.

77 Jagdish Bhagwati, *In Defense of Globalization* (Oxford: Oxford University Press, 2004), 172.

78 Bhagwati, *Explorations,* 191.

79 Ibid, 194.

80 John Maynard Keynes, *The Economic Consequences of the Peace* (New York: Harcourt, Brace & Howe, 1920), 11–12.

81 Martin, Fridson, "Twisted Tariffs," *Barrons* (July 26, 2004).

82 Niall Ferguson, *Chicago Tribune* (April 11, 2005): 3.

83 Paul Krugman, Paul, *The New York Times* (April 22, 2001).

84 David Brooks, *The New York Times*; cited in *Forbes* (January 31, 2005): 34.

Part Seven: Glaring Inequality

Chapter 14: Are There Alternatives to the Profit System?—Yes/No

85 R. Martin R. and R. Miller, R., *Economics* (Columbus, OH: Ohio State University Press, 1965), 9.

86 E. F. Schumacher, *Small is Beautiful: Economics as if People Mattered* (New York: Harper & Row, 1973), 36.

87 Ibid, 30.

88 *The New York Times* (January 30, 1995): B-5.

89 *In These Times* (December 8, 2003): 12.

90 *The New York Times* (September 26, 2004): A-21.

91 P. T. Bauer, *Equality, the Third World, and Economic Delusion* (Cambridge, MA: Harvard University Press, 1981), 9.

92 Ibid, 10.

93 J. Alsop, *I've Seen the Best of It* (New York: W. W. Norton & Company, 1992), 473.

Chapter 15: Should We Accept This Degree of Inequality?—No/Yes

94 Michael Harrington, *The Twilight of Capitalism* (New York: Simon and Schuster, 1976), 320.

95 David Gergen, *U.S. News and World Report* (May 14, 2001): 68.

96 John Maynard Keynes, *The General Theory of Employment, Interest, and Money* (London: Macmillan and Company, 1936), 374, 376.

97 Michael Harrington, *The Other America: Poverty in the United States* (New York: Penguin Books, 1981), 202.

98 Norman Cott, *The Free Market* (January 2003): 7.

99 *Forbe* (March 16, 1992): 64.

100 A World Bank estimate. See *World Development Report 2000/2001: Attacking Poverty* (Oxford, 2001); also cited in Rebecca Blank, *Is the Market Moral?: A Dialogue on Religion, Economics, and Justice* (Washington: Brookings Institution Press, 2004), 39.

101 Friedman, *Capitalism and Freedom*, 169.

102 Friedman, *Free to Choose*, 137.

103 Steve H. Hanke, "Kowtowing to Capitalism's Enemies," *Forbes* (August 6, 2001): 77.

104 Ibid.

105 Hazlitt, *Conquest of Poverty*, 51.

106 Arthur Okun, *Fortune* (November 1975): 199.

107 *Business Week* (August 12, 1985): 10.

108 Irving Kristol, "'Business' vs. 'The Economy,'" *The Wall Street Journal* (June 26, 1979): Op. Ed.

109 Ikeda, *Dynamics of the Mixed Economy*, 180.

110 *1994 Economic Report of the President*, President's Council of Economic Advisors.

Part Eight: Greed

Chapter 16: Does the Profit System Glorify Greed?—Yes

111 Wilhelm Röpke, *A Humane Economy: The Social Framework of the Free Market* (South Bend, IN: Gateway Editions, 1960), 113.

112 Denis Thomas, *The Mind of Economic Man* (Kent, UK: Quadrangle Books, 1970), 117.

113 Josephson, Matthew, *The Robber Barons: The Great American Capitalists, 1861–1901* (New York, 1934), vii–viii; also in Robert Bartley, *The Seven Fat Years: And How to Do It Again* (New York: Macmillan, 1992), 235.

114 *The Weekly Standard* (June 30, 2003): 19.

115 *The Weekly Standard* (February 25, 2002): 19.

116 Ibid.

117 *The Weekly Standard* (March 23, 1998): 38.

118 Marcia Angell, "The Truth About Drug Companies," *New York Review of Books* (July 15, 2004): 52.

119 *World Watch* (May/June 1997): 5.

Chapter 17: Does the Profit System Glorify Greed?—Yes, and a Good Thing

120 *New York Times Book Review* (September 26, 2004): 12.

121 Ralph Waldo Emerson, *Work and Days*; also in John Entwell, Murray Milgate, and Peter Newman, eds., *The New Palgrave: A Dictionary of Economics* (New York: Palgrave Publishers, 1998), vol. 4, 889.

122 *The Objectivist* Newsletter 2 (8): 31; also in Charles Robert McCann, ed., *The Elgar Dictionary of Economic Quotations* (Northampton, MA: Edward Elgar Publishing, 2003), 63.

123 John Maynard Keynes, *Essays in Persuasion* (New York: W. W. Norton & Company, 1963), 372.

124 Ayn Rand, *Atlas Shrugged* (New York: Signet Books, 1957), 415.

125 Ayn Rand, *Capitalism: The Unknown Ideal* (New York: Signet, 1967), 29.

126 Ibid, 28.

Chapter 18: Does the Profit System Glorify Greed?—No

127 Daniel Bell, *The Cultural Contradictions of Capitalism*, (New York: HarperCollins, 1976); quoted in Novak, *Spirit of Democratic Capitalism*, 171.

128 Friedman, *Capitalism and Freedom*, 164–65.

129 Adam Smith, *The Wealth of Nations* (Edinburgh, 1776), bk. 1, chap. 2, 20.

130 Ibid, bk. 4, 352.

131 David S. Landes, *The Wealth and Poverty of Nations: Why Some Are So Rich and Some So Poor* (New York: W. W. Norton & Company, 1999), 402.

132 Walter Lippmann, *The Good Society* (Boston: Little Brown and Company, 1943), 193–94; also in Novak, *Spirit of Democratic Capitalism*, 100.

133 Adam Smith, *Lectures*, 253–5; also in Cannan, *An Economist's Protest*, 425.

134 Adam Smith, *Moral Sentiments*, 464–6; also in Edwin Cannan, *An Economist's Protest*, 425.

135 Levy, *Profits and the Future*, 125.

136 George Stigler, *The Intellectual and the Market Place*, (1963); also in Thomas, *Mind of Economic Man*, 148.

137 Geoffrey Martin Hodgson, *Economics and Utopia* (1999), pt. III, 256; also in *Elgar Dictionary*, 75.

138 Letter to editor of Smith College campus newspaper, *Forbes*, July 21, 2003, 52.

139 Comment on "Does Studying Economics Inhibit Co-operation?" by Robert Frank, Thomas Gilovich, and Dennis Regan, in *Journal of Economic Perspectives* (Spring 1993), *The Economist*, n.d.

Part Nine: Government

Chapter 19: Can Government Protect Us from the Excesses of the Profit System?—Yes

140 Kenneth Hammond, "From Yao to Mao: 5,000 Years of Chinese History," New Mexico State University, taped lecture, The Teaching Company.

141 Ssu-Ma Ch'ien [now transliterated as Sima Qian] and Joseph J. Spengler, "Unsuccessful Exponent of Laissez-Faire," *Duke University Southern Economic Journal* (January 1964), 234.

142 Brewster, *New Essays on Trade*, 61; cited in Eli Heckscher, *Mercantilism* (London: George, Allen & Unwin Ltd., 1934), vol. 1, 318.

143 Smith, *Wealth of Nations*, bk. IV, ch. 5.

144 Landes, *Wealth and Poverty of Nations*, 327.

Chapter 20: Can Government Protect Us from the Excesses of the Profit System?—No

145 Keynes, *General Theory of Employment,* 351;: also quoted in Hazlitt, *Failure of the "New Economics,"* 184.

146 "From Yao to Mao," taped lecture.

147 Fernand Braudel, *Afterthoughts on Material Civilization and Capitalism* (Baltimore: The John Hopkins University Press, 1977), 73.

148 Ibid, p. 74.

149 Sakudo, *Management Practices*, 150–51, 154; cited in Landes, *Wealth and Poverty of Nations*, 362.

150 Thomas Macaulay, *History of England* (1848), vol. 1, chap. 3; quoted in Henry Hazlitt, *Economics in One Lesson* (San Francisco: Laissez Faire Books, 1996), 15.

151 *Grant's Interest Rate Observer* (December 6, 2002): 11.

152 Friedman, *Capitalism and Freedom*, 129.

153 See *The New York Times* (July 20, 2004): A-22; NPR's Evening Edition; and other sources.

154 Charles W. Cole, *French Mercantilism 1683–1700* (New York, 1943), 176; cited in Murray Rothbard, *Economic Thought Before Adam Smith: An Austrian Perspective on the History of Economic Thought*, volume I (Cheltenham, UK: Edward Elgar Publishing, 1999), 219.

155 Rothbard, *Economic Thought Before Adam Smith*, 270.

156 Jeremy Bentham, *Manual of Political Economy* (1798); also in Thomas, *Mind of Economic Man*, 196.

157 Mises, *Economic Policy*, 37.

158 Anne Robert Jacques Turgot, *Eloge de Gournay* (1770); also in Thomas, *Mind of Economic Man*, 158.

159 Entienne Bonnot, Abbé de Condillac, *Commerce and Government: Considered in their Mutual Relationship*, trans. Shelagh Eltis (Cheltenham, UK: Edward Elgar Publishing, 1997), 294.

160 *The Weekly Standard* (March 14, 2005): 40.

161 Michael Grunwald, *The Washington Post* (December 27, 2002): A-10.

162 D. Gwartney and Robert A Lawson, *Economic Freedom of the World* (1997); summarized in *Forbes* (June 16, 1997): 143.

163 Robert J. Barro and Xavier Sala-i-Martin, *Economic Growth* (New York, 1995), 434. ; also in Jasinowski, *Rising Tide*, 15.

164 David Dollar and Aart Kraay, "World Bank Study," *Forbes* (August 6, 2001): 77.

165 Israel Kirzner, *The Free Market* (February 2005): 7.

166 Aneurin Bevin, 1945 Labour Party Conference, in Thomas, *Mind of Economic Man*, 178.

167 Lippmann, *Good Society*, 119.

168 Mises, *Economic Policy*, 52.

169 Novak, *Spirit of Democratic Capitalism*, 19–20.

170 Ibid, afterword.

171 *Forbes* (November 25, 1991): 128.

172 *The New Yorker* (July 13, 2003): 98.

Part Ten: Central Banks

Chapter 21: Can Central Banks Protect Us from the Excesses of the Profit System and Lead the Economy? —Yes

173 *The Washington Post* (January 17, 1985): A-22.

174 Jeff Madrick, *The New York Review of Books* (May 3, 2001): 42.

175 *Forbes* (September 12, 2004): 127.

176 *Institutional Investor* Magazine (January 1988): 38.

177 Robert M. Solow, *The New Republic* (February 5, 2001): 28.

178 Sowell, *Basic Economics,* 287.

179 James Glassman, *The Washington Post* (April 11, 1995): A-21.

180 Merton Miller, *Institutional Investor* (September 1995): 59.

181 Paul McCulley, "Pacific Investment Management," *Fed Focus* (December 11, 2003): 4.

Chapter 22: Can Central Banks Protect Us from the Excesses of the Profit System and Lead the Economy? —No

182 *Deflation . . . What If,* Leuthold Group (December 2002).

183 *Business Week* (May 20, 1985): 38.

184 Murray Rothbard, *The Case Against the Fed* (Auburn, AL: Ludwig von Mises Institute, 1994), 11, 145.

185 M. Deane and R. Pringle, *The Central Bank* (London, 1994), n.p.; also in James Grant, *The Trouble with Prosperity: The Loss of Fear, the Rise of Speculation, and the Risk to American Savings* (New York: Times Books, 1996), 198.

186 G. Haberler, *The Austrian Theory of the Trade Cycle* (Auburn, AL: The Ludwig von Mises Institute, 1983), 7–8

187 Friedman, *Capitalism and Freedom*, 45.

188 Ibid, 44.

189 Jean-Baptiste Say, *Treatise*, 345–46; also in Holcombe, *15 Great Austrian Economists*, 53.

190 G. Epstein, interview, *The Austrian Economics Newletter* 20 (2): 8.

191 Callahan, *Economics for Real People*, 229.

192 Smith, *Wealth of Nations*, bk. IV, chap. 2; also in G. Bannock, R. E. Baxter, and R. Reef, *The Penguin Dictionary of Economics* (London: Penguin Books, 1972), 247.

193 Barbara Wootton, "The Necessity of Planning," in *The Burden of Plenty?* (1935); also in Thomas, *Mind of Economic Man*, 172.

194 R. Heilbroner, *The New Yorker* (January 23, 1989); also in Novak, *Spirit of Democratic Capitalism*, 417–18.

195 *The Economist* (September 20, 1997): 5.

196 Lindsey, *Against the Dead Hand*, xi.

197 J. Grant, interview, *The Austrian Economics Newsletter* 16, no 4 (Winter 1996): 2–3.

198 William Anderson, *The Free Market* (June 2003): 6.

199 Ned Davis Research, *Chart of the Day* (February 22, 2005), 1.

200 Ibid. (May 10, 2005), 1.

201 Callahan, *Economics for Real People*, 214–15.

202 "The Bank Credit Analyst," *The Outlook* (January 1996): 30.

203 Irving Kristol, *The Wall Street Journal* (July 24, 1978): op. ed.

204 Friedman, *Free to Choose*, 81.

205 *Grant's Interest Rate Observer* (February 27, 2004): 7.

206 For Krugman's comment, see *The New York Times* (May 20, 2005): A-25.

207 *Grant's Interest Rate Observer* (December 17, 2004): 11.

208 Marc Faber, *Tomorrow's Gold: Asia's Age of Discovery* (Hong Kong: CLSA Ltd., 2002), 346–47.

209 J Keynes, *General Theory*, 235.

210 Paul Kasriel, *Northern Trust Economic Research* (March 30, 2001).

211 Alexander Hamilton, Report to the House of Representatives, December 13, 1790, in American State Papers, Finance, 1st Congress, 3rd Session, no. 18, I, 67–76; also quoted in Jude Wanniski, *The Way the World Works: How Economies Fail—and Succeed* (New York: Basic Books, Inc., 1978), 204–05.

212 Ibid., 205.

213 Andrew Jackson, Farewell Address, March 4, 1837; also in George Seldes, *Great Thoughts* (New York: Ballantine Books, 1985), 202.

214 Alan Blinder, *Hard Heads, Soft Hearts* (1987); quoted in Samuelson, *The Washington Post* (September 7, 1994): A21.

215 *Forbes* (August 6, 2001): 77.

Part Eleven: Four Economic Value Systems

Competing Economic Value Systems

216 Alexander Skutch, *Life Ascending* (Austin: University of Texas Press, 1985), 218.

"Philanthropism"

217 Matthew 25: 42–43, 46.

218 Alexander Skutch, *Nature Through Tropical Windows* (Berkeley: University of California Press, 1983), 337–38.

Part Twelve: Reconciling Opposing Viewpoints

219 *Forbes* (September 6, 2004): 127.

220 Blank, Rebecca, *It Takes A Nation: A New Agenda for Fighting Poverty* (Princeton, 1997); also in Blank, *Is the Market Moral?*, 51.

221 Klein, Joe, *W* Magazine (September 16–23, 1991): 62.

222 *The Washington Post* (February 25, 1996): A-4.

223 Ibid.

224 Ted Rall, Yahoo News (September 13, 2005).

Appendices

Appendix One: What is a "Fair" Price?

225 Karl Marx and Friedrich Engels, *The German Ideology* (1845–46); and Karl Marx, *Criticism of the Gotha Programme* (1875).

226 For a good summary of objections to the labor theory of value, see Robert Nozick, *Anarchy, State and Utopia* (Cambridge: Harvard University Press, 1974).

Appendix Two: What Exactly Are Profits?

227 Levy, *Profits and the Future*, 132.

Appendix Three: Did the U.S. Congress Trigger the Stock Market Bubble of the Late 1990s?

228 See Bartley, *Seven Fat Years*, 257.

Index

D

I